CHRISTIAN HEROES: THEN & NOW

FLORENCE YOUNG

Mission Accomplished

CHRISTIAN HEROES: THEN & NOW

FLORENCE YOUNG

Mission Accomplished

JANET & GEOFF BENGE

P.O. BOX 55787 SEATTLE, WA 98155

YWAM Publishing is the publishing ministry of Youth With A Mission. Youth With A Mission (YWAM) is an international missionary organization of Christians from many denominations dedicated to presenting Jesus Christ to this generation. To this end, YWAM has focused its efforts in three main areas: (1) training and equipping believers for their part in fulfilling the Great Commission (Matthew 28:19), (2) personal evangelism, and (3) mercy ministry (medical and relief work).

For a free catalog of books and materials, call (425) 771-1153 or (800) 922-2143. Visit us online at www.ywampublishing.com.

Florence Young: Mission Accomplished
Copyright © 2005 by YWAM Publishing

Published by YWAM Publishing
a ministry of Youth With A Mission
P.O. Box 55787, Seattle, WA 98155

Fifth printing 2022

Library of Congress Cataloging-in-Publication Data
Benge, Janet, 1958–
  Florence Young : mission accomplished / Janet & Geoff Benge.
    p. cm. — (Christian heroes, then & now)
  Includes bibliographical references (p.   )
  ISBN 1-57658-313-9
  1. Young, Florence S. H., 1856–1940—Juvenile literature. 2. Missionaries—Australia—Biography—Juvenile literature. 3. Missionaries—Solomon Islands—Biography—Juvenile literature. 4. South Sea Evangelical Mission—Biography—Juvenile literature. I. Benge, Geoff, 1954–II. Title. III. Series.
  BV3705.Y68B46 2005
  266'.0092—dc22   2004023811

ISBN 978-1-57658-313-5 (paperback)
ISBN 978-1-57658-613-6 (e-book)

All rights reserved. No part of this book may be reproduced in any form without permission in writing from the publisher, except in the case of brief quotations in critical articles or reviews.

Printed in the United States of America

Christian Heroes: Then & Now

Adoniram Judson	Isobel Kuhn
Albert Schweitzer	Jacob DeShazer
Amy Carmichael	Jim Elliot
Betty Greene	John Flynn
Brother Andrew	John Newton
Cameron Townsend	John Wesley
Charles Mulli	John Williams
Clarence Jones	Jonathan Goforth
Corrie ten Boom	Klaus-Dieter John
Count Zinzendorf	Lillian Trasher
C. S. Lewis	Loren Cunningham
C. T. Studd	Lottie Moon
David Bussau	Mary Slessor
David Livingstone	Mildred Cable
Dietrich Bonhoeffer	Nate Saint
D. L. Moody	Norman Grubb
Elisabeth Elliot	Paul Brand
Eric Liddell	Rachel Saint
Florence Young	Richard Wurmbrand
Francis Asbury	Rowland Bingham
George Müller	Samuel Zwemer
Gladys Aylward	Sundar Singh
Helen Roseveare	Wilfred Grenfell
Hudson Taylor	William Booth
Ida Scudder	William Carey

Available in paperback, e-book, and audiobook formats. Unit study curriculum guides are available for select biographies.

www.YWAMpublishing.com

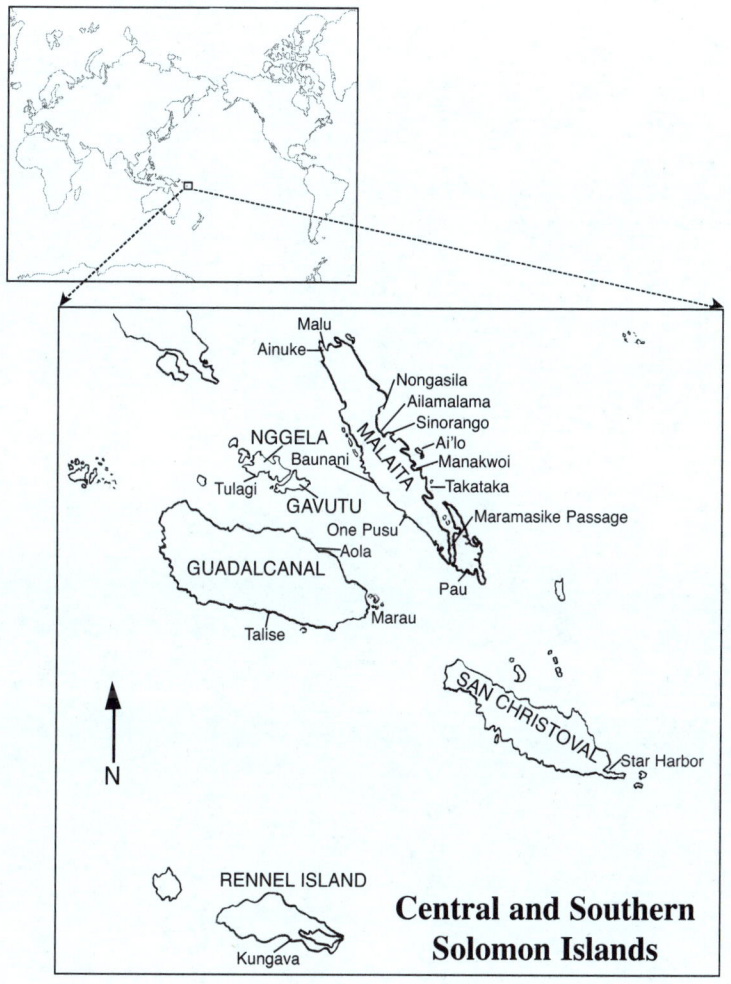

Contents

1. Becalmed 11
2. Erme Dale 15
3. A Colonial Girl 27
4. Changes 37
5. Kanakas 49
6. "Why Don't You Go?" 61
7. China. 71
8. "Not in Vain" 85
9. An-ren. 97
10. A New Direction 109
11. The Solomon Islands 121
12. The Eastern Side of the Island 133
13. The Cycle of Violence 145
14. A Growing Mission 155
15. Death and Hardship. 165
16. Her Real Legacy 179
    Bibliography 185

Chapter 1

Becalmed

"Reef to starboard," James Caulfeild yelled.

Florence Young glanced in the direction James pointed. There it was, a jagged coral reef waiting to gash the hull of the *Daphne* and toss those on board into the shark-infested water.

Florence watched as Owen Thomas, who was captaining the vessel, spun the wheel hard to port, but it was no use. There was no wind to fill the sails. They were becalmed and at the mercy of the ocean current carrying them toward the menacing reef. They were sailing just south of the equator, and during their three days at sea aboard the *Daphne,* there had been little wind. They should have been at their destination, the island of Gavutu, by now, but the island still lay many miles away across the tropical ocean.

Florence felt the stifling air close in around her, and her heart began to beat faster. "Lord, help us," she mumbled, holding the rigging firmly with both hands for support. She felt wretched; for hours now she had been standing clasping the rigging for support. She longed to lie down on the deck, but she was afraid that if she did, she might not get up again. Already two of her fellow missionaries, desperately ill with malaria, lay at her feet, one on either side of the small deck. Helen Fricke had a temperature of 106, while Hedley Abbott had a temperature of 104. As the fierce midday sun baked down on her, Florence felt as though her body were burning up and melting away at the same time. Her heart pounded and her head throbbed, but she willed herself to stay conscious. "Lord, help us," she prayed again.

As Florence prayed, James and three crew members from the island of Malu talked animatedly among themselves in pidgin English. At the same time, the men grabbed some of the lengths of lumber that were lying on the deck and tried to use them as paddles to maneuver the *Daphne* away from the reef. Their efforts were futile. The *Daphne* was much too heavy to be propelled by a few lengths of lumber.

Florence felt her knees begin to buckle, and she slumped into a hunched position on the deck. Hovering halfway between consciousness and oblivion, she continued praying through lips that barely moved now, "Lord, help us."

After several minutes Florence felt a gentle puff against her cheeks. Then she felt something tousle her hair. She opened her eyes and stared at the sail. It was beginning to flap. It was a breeze! But was it enough to pull the *Daphne* away from the reef to safety? Several more minutes passed before Florence had her answer. The sail finally began to billow, and she felt the boat start to be pulled along through the water, away from the reef. Florence breathed a sigh of relief and mumbled a short prayer of thanks.

The wind continued to blow for nearly half a day, carrying the *Daphne* along at a steady clip. Everyone on board was relieved. But as darkness began to descend over the boat, the wind dropped. The boat drifted throughout the night, and while Florence slept, the island crew members kept a sharp lookout in the moonlight for any more reefs.

As the sun climbed above the eastern horizon the next morning, it brought with it a gentle but steady breeze. Slowly but surely the *Daphne* again began inching its way toward Gavutu.

With the arrival of the new day, Florence willed herself to get up and assume her hunched position over the large box of sand on the deck of the *Daphne*. Pressed into the sand were two large tins, with a fire burning in each of them. Over the fire Florence boiled water for those aboard to drink and cooked rice for the crew to eat. In her malaria-weakened condition, it was grueling work, but she kept at it. She also tended to Helen and Hedley, who still lay on either side of the deck. Florence was also worried about Owen. The captain was not doing well either, but despite his raging fever, he resolutely kept his position behind the *Daphne*'s wheel.

Florence tried her best to rally everyone's spirits as the sun beat down on them, burning their skin and parching their mouths.

As darkness descended at the end of their fourth day at sea, Florence was glad to lie down and rest. But she was up with the sun the next morning, once again willing herself to keep going. By now, however, even she was beginning to wonder whether they would ever see land again.

To her great relief, in the late afternoon of their fifth day at sea, Florence could see Gavutu appear on the horizon. Her spirit soared. At last land was in sight. By then, however, Owen had lapsed into unconsciousness at the wheel, leaving James, with no sailing experience, and the makeshift native crew to guide the *Daphne* in failing light amid the reefs that guarded the harbor entrance on Gavutu. Finally, after grazing a reef with the keel of the boat, the men managed to moor the vessel alongside the dock.

Florence could hardly believe they had arrived safely. It was ten o'clock in the evening by then, and everyone aboard the *Daphne* was too exhausted to transfer to land. Florence collapsed right where she stood on the deck of the boat to sleep the night. As her fever-ravaged body drifted toward unconsciousness, her mind slipped back to her childhood and the unexpected twists and turns her life had taken to bring her to this place. The Solomon Islands were certainly a long way from the South Island of New Zealand, where she had been born. What would the people who had known her there think of this latest adventure she found herself in the middle of?

Chapter 2

Erme Dale

Four-year-old Florence Young stood holding her younger sister Constance by the hand on the deck of the *Anglesea,* an old sailing sloop. She waited beside their old family maid Elizabeth, just as her mother had told her to. Florence scarcely knew in what direction to look first. Passengers, hat boxes and carpetbags in hand, were streaming up the gangplank. Some dabbed their eyes with handkerchiefs, while others waved bravely at the crowd standing on the London dock.

Florence caught glimpses of her family too. Her mother was following two sailors who were carrying the family's big leather trunk to their cabin. And two of her older brothers, Ernest and Horace, and her older sister Emily were busy carrying boxes and suitcases down to their cabin.

As Florence watched the scene, she tried hard to recall all she could about the trip from the British colony of New Zealand to England two years before. She was only two years old then, but some things were burned into her memory. She recalled the way her father had to help the captain man the ship when the first and second mates both ran off to join the gold rush on the west coast of the South Island of New Zealand. She also recalled how things had become desperate when the captain accidentally sailed too far south, into the ice floes that broke off from Antarctica. She had never felt so cold in her life. Icicles hung from the rigging, and the deck was so slick that the children were forbidden to go topside for three weeks, until they reached warmer water.

Fear raced through Florence's mind as she stood on the deck of the *Anglesea*. Would the trip back to New Zealand be as perilous as the trip to England had been? This time her father wouldn't even be with them. He and her oldest brother, Arthur, and a cousin, William McAdam, had traveled to New Zealand ahead of the rest of the family to prepare for their arrival. Why, Florence wondered, did her family have to go back to New Zealand at all? Everyone she loved—her four grandparents and her numerous aunts, uncles, and cousins—all lived in England. It was impossible to imagine why her own family had to follow her father halfway around the world to start out again on a farm in the middle of nowhere.

Florence did not dare tell her mother how she felt. As long as Florence could remember, her mother had been a sickly person, and Florence did not like to burden her mother with complaints. During the eleven-week voyage to New Zealand, she tried hard to be a good girl, reading aloud to Constance, playing endless games of checkers with her older brothers, and doing her reading and arithmetic lessons with Emily.

Thankfully, the January voyage was uneventful, and warm, since they sailed from the Northern to the Southern Hemisphere, exchanging midwinter for midsummer.

Finally the rugged coastline of South Island came into view on the horizon. Lush green native forest stretched away from the seashore, and in the distance Florence could see the majestic peaks of the Southern Alps stretching into the clear summer air. At last, on February 1, 1861, the voyage from England was over and the *Anglesea* arrived in Dunedin, New Zealand. Dunedin had been founded thirteen years earlier by Scottish settlers and was a fast-growing city. With its stone and brick buildings, it reminded Florence of an English town. However, it was not their final destination. The Young family boarded a smaller steamer that took them to Bluff, a town on the extreme southern tip of South Island. There Florence's father, Henry, along with her brother Arthur and cousin William, met the ship.

Tears gathered in Florence's eyes as she hugged her father. She had missed him so much. Soon his powerful hands were heaving the family's trunks and suitcases onto a wagon for the tortuous journey inland. As her brothers loaded the wagon, Florence's father explained that he had bought a farm near Riverton. To get there they would have to travel north to Invercargill and then head west twenty miles to Riverton. From there they would head ten miles inland to the family's new homestead called Erme Dale.

Even though it was still summer in New Zealand, the track they traveled on was muddy, and the wagon became bogged down many times. Florence was surprised by how different the scenery was from that in England, where thatched cottages and stone dairies dotted the landscape and the farms were divided by neat hedgerows. Now, except for the wagon ruts in the mud, it seemed like they went for miles without seeing another sign of human life. On her left Florence looked out across Foveaux Strait, which divided South Island from Stewart Island farther to the south. On her right was dense native forest that stretched inland as far as she could see. Beautiful fantails and wood pigeons flitted among the trees.

As they rode along, Florence's father explained that New Zealand had no native mammals or snakes and that nothing was lurking in the bush that could harm them. Florence was greatly relieved to hear this, because the thick beach forests and flax marshes looked scary to her.

It took the family three days to reach their new home. Along the way they had to cross three rivers: the Oreti, the Waimatuku, and the Purakino. They had to load the horses and wagon onto a large punt to be ferried across the Oreti River.

Finally they reached Erme Dale, and Florence joined the older boys as they jumped off the wagon and rushed to get a look inside their new home. Much to their surprise, the house was not finished. The square hall was filled with wood shavings, and the staircase had only three steps nailed in place. And when Horace lit the stove in the dining room, the house immediately filled with smoke, sending the children spluttering out of the house. Their father explained that he was having difficulty getting someone to cart fire bricks from Invercargill to the new house, so until the bricks arrived and the fireplace was finished, they could not use it.

Family life soon settled into a routine that left Florence and Constance with a lot of time to explore their strange new surroundings. At first the two small girls were reluctant to be out of sight of the house, but with each adventure they became braver. Soon the Dripping Well was one of their favorite places to go. The Dripping Well was a limestone cave at the head of a gully. It contained a pool of crystal clear water surrounded by moss and ferns. Rocky Island Bush, which surrounded the cave, also became a favorite haunt. Among the yellow-and-green-striped flax and the bracken of the bush were weird-shaped, giant-sized boulders. Fueled with images of fairytales, Florence and Constance turned various rocks into castles and fortresses and spent hundreds of happy hours among the rocks, making up intricate stories.

As autumn arrived, the nearby beach forest turned deep red and the leaves carpeted the ground.

Winter, though, was much colder than Florence imagined it would be. Snow settled on the ground in June. The fire bricks had not yet arrived, and so all of the cooking had to be done outside over an open fire. Sometimes the wind was so cold that the adults and older children had to take turns tending to their dinner as it cooked. The diet was monotonous: rice, dried apples from America, and salted beef and pickled pork from England. How Florence longed for the foamy milk and yellow butter she had eaten in England. Even the thought of fresh cauliflower or cabbage began to appeal to her.

Henry Young assured his family that things would be different next year. They would plant vegetables in the spring and buy a cow to provide milk, cream, and cheese for them.

Since no neighbors were within walking distance, it was unusual to see visitors. But anyone who did venture as far as Erme Dale was met with kind hospitality. Florence loved it when visitors came, as they often brought books and newspapers and told stories of what was happening in other parts of New Zealand or in the home country, England.

There was, however, one visitor Florence had mixed feelings about. Mr. Honare was a native New Zealander, or Maori. Like Florence's parents, Mr. Honare belonged to the Plymouth Brethren denomination. He was an evangelist who walked much of the southern part of South Island preaching to the Maori people. Florence did not have any problems with that. What she didn't like was the way Mr. Honare and her parents talked about how they were ready to meet Jesus and how wonderful that would be. Although Florence had heard such conversations before, she hated it when Mr. Honare prayed for them all and asked Jesus to come back and take them to heaven. "How selfish he is," she told herself. "He might want Jesus to come back, but what about me? I'm not ready to meet Him."

To Florence's relief, Mr. Honare always kept his visits short. Florence tried to forget about how uncomfortable his prayers made her feel, and plenty of other things were going on at Erme Dale to distract her from Mr. Honare's visits. For one, her older sister Emily was getting married to a man from Invercargill. His name was John Deck, and he was a doctor. With everyone caught up in preparations for the first wedding in the family, the day was quickly upon them. The wedding was held in the family living room, and then in a big flourish of hugs and kisses, Emily was gone, leaving Florence as the oldest daughter in the house.

Suddenly, at eight years old, Florence had a whole new set of responsibilities. It was now her job to sit at the end of the table and pour the tea and to make breakfast for everyone. Her mother, whose health was failing, did not come downstairs until nearly lunchtime each day. By then the breakfast dishes were done and lunch preparation well under way.

In late September, Florence's mother announced that she needed to go to Invercargill. Florence's heart beat fast. She knew her ninth birthday was coming up and that her mother would be planning to buy her a present in town. After much begging, it was decided that Florence, her older brother Ernest, and their cousin Willie McAdam would be allowed to make the journey with Mrs. Young.

The following morning Willie hitched the family's two horses, Blackbird and Blossom, to the wagon, and Ernest helped Mrs. Young up into the front seat. Ernest and Florence sat in the back of the wagon, while Willie sat next to Mrs. Young to drive the horses. A slap of the reins started the two faithful animals on the long trek to town.

They made good time to Riverton, where they stopped to visit some friends. Then it was off again on the journey to Invercargill. It was low tide, and the fastest way to travel at low tide was along the beach. Willie headed the wagon onto the wide, windswept beach, and soon they were rolling along over the hard, glistening, gray sand. There had been a storm the night before, and the day was damp and dreary. The sea, whipped to a frenzy by the wind, crashed against the beach. The wind tousled Florence's hair as she watched the seabirds circling over the beach. They reached the Waimatuku River, which was shallow and easily forded at low tide, and crossed over it. Then they drove on farther down the beach, all the while looking for the sign that marked the way for wagons to leave the beach and pass through a gap in the low sand hills and rejoin the road to Invercargill. They had gone several miles when Willie began to voice his concern that perhaps they had missed the turnoff. He turned the wagon around and headed back the way they had come, looking for the marker. But they could not spot it. Eventually Willie satisfied himself that he had not missed the marker, and once again he turned the wagon around and headed back down the beach.

As the sun began to sink low on the horizon, Willie became convinced that they had indeed missed the marker. They needed to find it, because for the next thirty-two miles there was no place where a wagon could be driven off the beach, and already the tide was well on its way in. Willie guided the wagon into the loose, dry sand at the top of the beach above the high-tide line and brought it to a halt. He jumped down from the wagon and headed off along the beach on foot, promising to return when he had found the place where they should turn off. The three Youngs stayed with the wagon and horses. Florence sat on a log on the beach, snuggled up to her mother, to wait.

It was eleven o'clock at night before Willie returned. He had found the signpost. It had been blown down in the storm the night before and lay flat and half buried in the sand. They would have to backtrack six miles along the beach until they came to the turnoff point.

The night air was cold and damp, and fog had begun to form along the beach. Florence huddled in the back of the wagon and pulled her woolen coat tight around her for warmth as they rolled along.

Eventually Willie found the turnoff and guided the wagon off the beach and onto the muddy track that served as the road to Invercargill. Finally, at three in the morning, the wagon made its way down the deserted streets of the town.

After several hours of sleep, Florence set out with her mother to go shopping. They bought a number of supplies for Erme Dale, including several new books and some newspapers for Mr. Young. Then her mother bought a doublewide slate as a present for Florence's birthday. Florence was delighted with the gift. She would be able to write her school lessons on the slate, which was big enough for her to draw some wonderful pictures too.

The following morning Ernest and Willie loaded up the wagon for the trip back to Erme Dale. Florence's new slate was packed away in a box with a collection of large corks that Mrs. Young planned to use to stop the tops of the jars of preserves she would make from the fruits and vegetables planted in the new garden at Erme Dale.

As they drove along, Florence noticed that Blackbird was unusually frisky this morning. He was hard to rein in and kept pulling against Blossom, the other horse. When they reached the Oreti River, they waited for the punt to cross over to pick them up and ferry them across the river. Mrs. Young was tired from all the travel and the whirlwind of shopping in Invercargill and wanted to stay seated on the wagon during the crossing. But Ernest reminded her that Mr. Young forbade anyone to stay on the wagon while it crossed the river, fearing it was too dangerous, and managed to coax his mother down. Willie guided the horses and wagon onto the deck of the punt, and they set out across the Oreti.

They were not yet halfway across when Blackbird seemed determined to take a drink from the river. He lunged forward. Blossom tried to pull against him but eventually gave in. The two horses careened forward, with the wagon following. Seeing what was happening, Willie grabbed his knife and frantically tried to cut the leather traces that held the horses to the wagon. But it was too late; horses and wagon tumbled off the front of the punt and splashed into the cold, clear water of the Oreti River.

As frantically as Ernest and Willie and the ferryman tried, there was little they could do. Coughing and snorting and churning up the water, the horses heaved desperately against the weight of the wagon. They lunged and kicked, but with the wagon pulling on them, Blackbird and Blossom soon drowned. The contents of the wagon spilled into the river and sank to the bottom, and the water stilled.

Florence could scarcely believe what she had just witnessed. Everything was gone, even the new slate that was to be her birthday present. She wanted to cry about it and then realized she needed to be strong for her mother's sake.

When the punt reached the other side of the river, Ernest and Willie, with the help of the ferryman, tried to salvage what they could. The wagon had sunk wheels first to the bottom of the river. The men were able to attach a rope to the wagon and, after cutting the drowned horses free, dragged it from the water. They were also able to collect a number of the larger, heavier items from the river bottom and load them back onto the wagon, but the books and newspapers for Mr. Young were completely ruined.

While the men worked, Florence walked along the edge of the river. There, she found some comfort when, to her delight, she spotted the box containing her new slate bobbing in the water at the edge of the river. The corks in the box had kept it afloat, and the current had pushed it to the edge. Florence scooped up the box and excitedly ran to show her mother.

Finally, using two borrowed horses, the group made it back to Erme Dale. It had been quite an adventure, and soon Florence was sitting beside her father telling him all about the trip while he drank a cup of strong black tea.

October 10, 1865, was Florence's ninth birthday. It was also her father's birthday. After receiving her slate, wrapped in brown paper, for her birthday present, Florence and the rest of the family made their way to Rocky Island Bush for a picnic. Back at the house following the picnic, they pushed aside the furniture in the front room and everyone joined in a game of blindman's bluff.

Florence enjoyed a wonderful birthday, and as she went to sleep that night, she wondered what surprises the year ahead might hold for her.

Chapter 3

A Colonial Girl

The following year Florence was surprised when her father announced that he had sold Erme Dale and the family would be moving into Invercargill. Her surprise turned to delight when Florence learned that her married sister Emily, who lived in Invercargill, was expecting a baby.

Henry Young found a small house in town for the family to rent, and they moved just in time for the birth of Emily's baby. It was a girl, whom they named Kathleen. Florence was thrilled to be an aunt at ten years of age, and she spent many hours helping her older sister with the baby. Everything seemed perfect until her father announced that he could not make a living in Invercargill and the family would have to move to Australia.

Florence's father and brothers went on ahead of the rest of the family to find a place in Australia to settle down in. Like New Zealand, Australia was home to many British colonists. Letters passed between the divided family, and Florence learned that her father had chosen to settle near Melbourne, on the southeastern end of the continent. From the way her father and brothers described Australia, Florence was sure that she would not like it. The place sounded dry and barren compared to New Zealand, and her brothers wrote about snakes, dangerous crocodiles, and other strange reptiles. Florence wept when it was time to leave Invercargill, and she made Emily promise to come and visit as soon as she could.

Dromana, the small community located forty-five miles south of Melbourne, was even more disappointing than Florence had imagined it would be. The family arrived in March 1868, and everyone was set to work in the new family venture—growing grapes. Within a week eleven-year-old Florence had learned to loathe the vineyard her father and brothers had planted when they first arrived on the property.

Florence and Constance were given the job of killing the caterpillars that munched their way through the grape leaves. They lost count of how many hundreds of them they squashed in a day, and much to their dismay, there seemed to be a never-ending supply of them. Florence looked forward to the end of the growing season, when she could go and swim at the nearby beach at Port Philip.

Over time Florence began to adjust to her new life in Australia. She even found things about it she enjoyed. Her mother seemed healthier in the hot climate and got out a lot more. Mrs. Young made friends with an old woman who lived five miles away at Red Hills. The woman's name was Mrs. Evans, and she soon became a grandmother figure to Florence and her siblings.

There were no libraries in the area, but Mrs. Evans loaned the children all kinds of books. Florence's favorite books were the ones written by Sir Walter Scott. Along with the books, Mrs. Evans provided white rabbits and canaries for pets, and a pony that she allowed Florence to keep for six months. Florence discovered that she loved to ride, and she became an expert at catching and saddling the pony.

Just as it had been in New Zealand, there was no school nearby for the children to attend, so a neighbor came once or twice a week to help the children with their schoolwork.

When they had been in Australia for two years, Emily came to visit from Invercargill. She now had two children, Kathleen and baby Connie. Sadly, the visit turned into a disaster when Emily came down with typhoid fever soon after she arrived. Her husband, Dr. John Deck, made a hasty trip across the Tasman Sea to Australia to nurse Emily, and everyone was relieved when she began to recover.

About this time Florence overheard several conversations that made her realize the vineyard was not making enough money to support the family.

She was secretly delighted when she heard her father explaining that he was going to sell the property and return to New Zealand.

Sure enough, after an absence of three years, the Young family did pack up and move back to New Zealand. Florence's happiness at being back on South Island had an element of surprise as she found herself living in a large canvas tent on a remote sheep station at Otapiri, in the Hokonui Hills, about twenty miles from Erme Dale, the old family farm.

While Florence's father made plans to build a house on the new farm for his family, some good news arrived. Florence's Uncle Charles, her father's oldest brother, who was a wealthy merchant in England, offered to buy Erme Dale back from its new owners and arrange things so that her brothers Arthur and Horace could farm the place. Still more good news arrived. Word came that Florence's mother's brother, Dr. William Eccles, and his family had emigrated from England to Dunedin, about seventy miles away. However, Florence's joy in her newly reunited family was short-lived.

When her parents learned that Uncle William was taking his own children back to England to be educated, they decided that it was time that fourteen-year-old Florence had some formal schooling as well. What a wonderful opportunity, they told her, to travel back to England with her cousins and settle into a school there.

Time passed quickly, and on April 5, 1871, Florence found herself on her fifth ocean voyage.

This time she was traveling on the *Spirit of Dunedin*, a ship that carried New Zealand's chief export, wool, to the markets in England and Europe. Florence soon found out that nothing about a wool ship was glamorous. The food was greasy and cold, and each passenger was allotted just two pints of cold, rust-colored water a day to bathe and wash his or her clothes in. In addition, there were no ports of call along the way, and the eighty-four-day voyage seemed like an eternity.

At last Florence spotted land: Start Point on the Isle of Wight. What a welcome sight it was after seeing nothing but blue sea and sky for nearly three months.

During the voyage Florence had tried not to think about what might happen when she arrived at school. She knew she loved to read, but she had little idea about geometry, Latin, or French. Her stomach turned into knots when she contemplated going to class with other fourteen-year-olds. Would she look like a fool? Would they guess that she had never been to school? Florence decided that no matter how hard she had to work, she would catch up to the other students.

Florence and her cousins were met at the dock in England by two of her mother's sisters, Annie and Julia. The women were both so short that the children soon dubbed them their "Little Aunts."

The Little Aunts gave everyone a warm welcome and took them all back to their nicely furnished house at Sydenham, where seven servants were ready and waiting to tend to their needs. Compared to the tent on the new family farm in New Zealand, the house and servants in England almost seemed like a dream to Florence, who was to spend the two months until school started in this wonderful place with her aunts.

From the Little Aunts' house at Sydenham, it was not far to her Grandfather Young's estate, situated on the River Thames between Maidenhead and Cookham. Florence went to visit her father's family there. She had vague memories of the place from ten years before. While it looked like a three-story castle from the outside, the basement windows were shaped like a ship's portholes, and the flat roof resembled a quarterdeck. Admiral Sir George Young, Florence's great-grandfather, had built the place, designing it to remind him of his life at sea. While Florence's great-grandfather had spent his life at sea, her grandparents had a long association with India. In fact, Florence's father had been born in India and served as the youngest judge in the colony before marrying her mother. Echoes of India filled Grandmother and Grandfather Young's house, from the intricately carved trunk in the bedroom to the bright orange silk drapes in the parlor. And Florence loved it when her grandfather and uncles told her stories about their adventures in India. It stirred her imagination and reminded her of her father.

After nine carefree weeks staying with the Little Aunts, it was time to start boarding school in Blackheath, near Greenwich in London. The first weeks at school were the most difficult for Florence. She did her best to fit in with the other girls, though she was acutely aware that she was a colonial girl with a different accent and a sense of independence born of living and working on the land in New Zealand and Australia.

Most of the teachers gave lectures, during which the students took notes and then reconstructed them into written reports about what they had learned. Florence had never listened so hard or written so much in her life, and she soon realized that the three hours of silence after dinner each night were not enough both to complete all her homework and to study to catch up with her classmates. She got into the habit of getting up in the morning when it was still dark, dressing, and making her bed. Then she would sit quietly until the first rays of sunlight burst through the eastern window of the dormitory room. That was her signal to begin studying.

It was a grueling routine, but Florence stuck to it. And as the year rolled by, she not only caught up to the other girls academically but also passed them. By the end of the year, Florence was top of her class, and she was top of it the following year as well.

Everyone agreed that Florence had done exceptionally well at school, but the opportunities for an educated girl in England were limited. She could become a schoolteacher, or perhaps a governess, but Florence did not care for either profession. In October 1873, with her schooling behind her, Florence Young boarded a ship to return to New Zealand.

The long and arduous journey back home took 106 days. For eleven days the ship was becalmed in the English Channel, and during the rest of the voyage, they encountered only light winds. The ship reached Melbourne, Australia, on January 20, 1874, where Florence transferred to a steamer for the continuation of the journey to Bluff, New Zealand. In Bluff, Florence's brother Arthur met her, and the two of them went by train to Invercargill and then on to Winton, where they caught a stagecoach to Flint's Crossing. Horace was waiting for them at Flint's Crossing with three horses, and the three siblings rode the last thirteen miles over the hills to Otapiri on horseback.

Florence loved every moment of her journey home across the wild southern landscape of South Island. She had not ridden a horse for nearly three years, and she loved the feeling of freedom as the animal galloped along. She also enjoyed being flanked by her brothers again.

When Florence had left for England, there had been only a tent on the new farm at Otapiri. Now, as she galloped onto the property, she saw that a small wooden house had replaced the tent. Like every other house she had passed on the train and stagecoach trip, the new house was rectangular, with a steeply sloped roof and a veranda running the full length of the front. A chimney rose at one side. In the field in front of the house, a mob of sheep was clustered among the cabbage trees.

Florence's mother and father were waiting on the veranda as she and her brothers rode up. After many hugs and greetings all around, Florence was ushered inside to inspect the family's new home.

Inside the front door were two small living rooms, and then a bedroom. The kitchen was a lean-to off the back of the house. A steep staircase led up to two attic bedrooms, whose sloping walls had been papered with pictures from the *Illustrated London News*. As Mrs. Young proudly showed off her handiwork, Florence was overwhelmed with what her parents had given up to be pioneers in New Zealand. Back in England her relatives lived a pampered life with butlers, parlor maids, and coachmen, but out here in the colonies, her parents had to do everything for themselves.

That evening, as Florence sat with her family on the veranda, she understood the pull this place could have on people. From her perch she gazed out across the Waimea Plains to the barren hills beyond. In the twilight, the shadows cast by the hills produced fantastic shapes. And behind the barren foothills towered the majestic snow-covered Southern Alps. Florence took in the sight and breathed deeply. It felt so good to be home again.

Chapter 4

Changes

Over the next day or so, Florence caught up on all of the family news. Constance was away at boarding school in Dunedin, and Emily had given birth to two more children while Florence was away in England. Florence was delighted to learn that Emily and the four children would be visiting in February. However, when they arrived, the news was not good.

Florence's brother-in-law John had been kicked in the knee by a horse the previous winter, and the joint had not healed. In fact, it had become so painful that Dr. John had given up his busy medical practice because he needed bed rest. The Young family rallied around to help, and it was decided that Florence should join Arthur and Horace at Erme Dale and that the six members of the Deck clan should join them there for the fall and winter. The Erme Dale house was larger than the one her parents lived in at Otapiri and was better suited to a large influx of visitors. Florence loved Erme Dale and did not mind going there to help out. She enjoyed getting to know her new niece Emily, or Emmie, as everyone called her, and her nephew Harry.

Fall and winter passed quickly, but as spring rolled around, John was no better. A family meeting was held, and it was decided that John should return to England for an operation. Emily would go with him and take the two oldest children, Kathleen and Constance, with her. The two youngest children would stay with Florence.

In September Florence accompanied her sister to Dunedin, where the Deck family now lived, to help with the depressing task of disposing of or packing up the family's furniture and belongings.

On her first Saturday in Dunedin, Florence went to the local Plymouth Brethren prayer meeting with her sister. From the moment she stepped into the hall, Florence felt like she had when Mr. Honare had visited the family at Erme Dale. Her stomach turned to knots, and as she listened to a Brethren elder preach, she became convinced that tonight was the night she must become a Christian. When the meeting was over, Emily introduced her to the speaker, Albert Brunton.

"Would you like to break bread with us tomorrow?" Mr. Brunton asked.

Florence did not know what to say. She had heard that a person should publicly acknowledge that Christ was his or her Savior and be baptized before taking communion, something Florence had never done.

"But," she stammered, "how could I? Aren't I supposed to be baptized first?"

Mr. Brunton smiled. "You do love the Lord, don't you?" he asked.

As she thought about his question, a surge of confidence flooded through Florence. "Yes, I do," she replied.

"Then wouldn't you like to meet with us at His table?"

"Yes, I would, if I may," Florence said.

The following morning Florence went to the morning service with Emily and took communion. She felt a new freedom like she had never experienced before. A week later Mr. Brunton baptized Florence.

Florence's eighteenth birthday soon rolled around, and her father arrived with a beautifully bound copy of Bagster's Bible for a birthday gift. Florence knew she would treasure it for the rest of her life.

It took six weeks to pack up the Deck home. When the job was done, Florence knew it was time to head home again. Spring had settled over the countryside, and lambing season was in full swing. At the end of October, Florence boarded the three-hundred-ton steamer *Wanganui* for the trip to Bluff.

The steamer left on Wednesday morning and would arrive in Bluff at daybreak the next morning—that is, if everything went according to schedule, which it did not.

The trip started out normally enough. The *Wanganui* was filled with more than one hundred passengers, including many poor Scottish people hoping to make a living off the rugged New Zealand landscape. Florence had bought herself a berth in the ladies' cabin, which she shared with seven other women and a stewardess. Those passengers who did not have berths slept on the benches and tables in the saloon. But as it turned out, no one slept at all that night.

A furious gale blew up as the ship headed south. The *Wanganui* pitched and rolled in the churning sea, making most on board sick. When the vessel rounded Cape Saunders, the gale became so fierce that the ship was forced to seek shelter behind a reef lest it be swamped by the roiling waves. It took two anchors to hold the ship in place against the onslaught. The time of their arrival in Bluff came and went, and they were still stuck in the storm. After another day and night, the ship was still huddled behind the reef. By now all the food supplies on board had been used up, and the captain was worried. He had used up so much coal fighting against the storm that he did not have enough fuel to return to Dunedin and wait out the storm in the confines of the harbor there. All they could do was stay at anchor behind the reef and hope and pray that the storm would abate soon.

The next day one of the anchor chains holding the *Wanganui* snapped, and the vessel began to drift precariously close to the rocky reef. The captain did his best to keep the ship afloat and off the rocks, but the storm still howled.

Finally, the following day, the winds began to abate, and the *Wanganui* was able to resume its journey to Bluff. But the going was still slow, and they did not reach Bluff until Sunday morning. The voyage had turned into a four-day nightmare, and Florence was very relieved to once again have her feet on dry land.

Arthur was waiting with a covered wagon to meet his sister in Bluff. He explained to Florence that the weather was now so beautiful that he had decided they should make a camping expedition of their journey back to Erme Dale. Florence was delighted, and they set off along the coast.

They set a leisurely pace, and it took them three days to get to Erme Dale. While Florence had been in Dunedin helping Emily pack, her parents and Emily's two younger children had moved back into the house at Erme Dale, and Horace, Ernest, and Constance, who had returned from boarding school, had moved into the house at Otapiri. Mrs. Young was pleased to see her daughter again. She had been looking after her husband, who was ill with the flu. Within a couple of days of Florence's return, Mr. Young started feeling better.

No sooner had Mr. Young recovered than an urgent message arrived from Otapiri. Horace was dangerously ill with pneumonia and wanted his mother and Florence to come at once to look after him.

Mr. Young agreed to look after Emily's two younger children, and the women left that evening. Arthur drove them through the night in the covered wagon to Invercargill, where Florence and her mother arrived in time to catch the morning train to Winton. There they hired horses and rode the rest of the way to Otapiri. During the trip Florence was concerned about her mother, who had never been a strong person. The lack of comfort and sleep made her mother seem especially fragile.

Ernest and Connie were relieved when the two travelers finally arrived. Horace was very ill. A doctor from Invercargill had made two visits and had just pronounced that Horace must be moved into town, where he could be attended to every day.

There was no road at Otapiri, and since Horace was too ill to mount a horse and ride, he had to be carried over the hills on a stretcher. It was the longest thirteen miles Florence had ever walked. The weather turned cold on the first night, and they stopped at the home of a neighboring farmer. Snow fell heavily during the night, and they were totally snowed in. It was three days before they were able to get on their way again.

When they arrived in Invercargill, the family rented rooms in a boardinghouse. Horace's room was the only one with a fireplace in it, and everyone huddled together around the fire for fear that they too might catch pneumonia from the cold. Florence's mother did come down with the illness. Mr. Young arrived from Erme Dale with Emily's two children to visit just before the doctor pronounced his diagnosis.

It was just after eight o'clock in the evening when the doctor left the boardinghouse. After he had gone, Mr. Young took Florence aside. "The doctor has spoken privately with me," he began. "He says that your mother does not have the strength to fight the disease and that she probably won't live till morning."

Florence stared at her father. She heard the words he said, but she could not believe them. She and her mother had come to nurse Horace. If anyone was near death, it was he, not her mother!

Mrs. Young had been ill many times before, and Florence was convinced that she would make a slow recovery as she always had. However, she did not. Florence's mother died two hours later.

Florence stared into the lifeless face of her mother. She could hardly think about what had happened, much less what to do next. A quiet family funeral followed three days later. Horace did not attend, as he hovered between life and death himself.

Following the funeral Florence returned to nursing her brother. It was a lonely vigil without her mother at her side. Two doctors confirmed that Horace was indeed dying. But this time the doctors' predictions proved incorrect. Horace began to make a slow recovery, and six weeks later he returned with the rest of the family to Erme Dale.

Florence found that the house at Erme Dale was now filled with sad memories for her. It was difficult for her to imagine a bright and happy future without her mother around. She grew depressed and became even more so when a year later Emily and John Deck arrived back in Invercargill. While in England Emily had given birth to a fifth baby, a son whom they named Northcote. With their return, Florence knew it was time for her sister's family to be reunited. But she had grown to love her two little charges and hated to see them move back into town to be with their parents. Constance left Erme Dale at the same time to finish her education in England, and Mr. Young moved to Invercargill to pursue a business scheme. With Horace and Ernest now back at Otapiri, only Florence and Arthur were left at Erme Dale. And when Arthur was away visiting the far reaches of the farm, Florence found herself alone at Erme Dale for up to two weeks at a time.

For any nineteen-year-old girl this would be a lonely existence, but for Florence, who was still trying to recover from the death of her mother, it was almost intolerable. And when she learned that Emily, John, and their five children were moving to Sydney, Australia, she could hardly bear to think about it. One thing, however, managed to turn Florence's attention from her own loneliness: rabbits, hundreds of thousands of them, perhaps even millions. Rabbits were not native to New Zealand. Early English settlers who thought it would be nice to go rabbit hunting had introduced them into the country. Regrettably, they did not realize until too late that the rabbits had no natural enemies in New

Zealand, as they did in England. As a result the rabbit population in New Zealand was soon wildly out of control. Rabbits grazed on the grass, the same grass that was meant to feed cows and sheep. Often they came through like locusts, eating every blade of grass and causing erosion on the hillsides.

Florence watched in frustration as her brothers tried everything that they could think of to rid their farms of the pest. They poisoned the rabbits, shot them, and made traps for them, but nothing seemed to have an impact on the rabbit population.

Like many other homesteaders, Florence's father and brothers had no option in the end but to send their livestock away to be slaughtered and walk off the land. With all the grass gone, there was no point in staying at the farms.

A family conference was held in Invercargill, and it was decided that both Erme Dale and Otapiri should be sold and that Florence, her father, and her three brothers should all emigrate to Australia once again.

Florence hoped it was the right move. She was tired of living in different countries, but she was cheered by the idea of being on the same continent as Emily and John and the children.

In 1878 Florence moved to Invercargill while Arthur and Horace went on ahead in search of a suitable investment in Australia. She eagerly awaited each letter her brothers wrote and followed their journey through New South Wales and Queensland. They had been gone just over a year when Arthur wrote to say that they had bought land near Bundaberg, about two hundred miles north of Brisbane in Queensland. It was ideal land for growing sugarcane, which was a very profitable crop.

Florence was relieved to know where she was finally going to settle in Australia. However, her father had some business to attend to in England, and so in early 1880 he and Florence and Ernest set out for England together. They traveled aboard the liner *Deccan*. On the way, the ship docked in Bombay, India, for seven days. Florence was excited about the stop. All her life she had heard her father's stories about his childhood in India and his years as a judge. Now, finally, she got to explore her father's old haunts.

They started by visiting the Hill Station of Matheran, where Florence and Ernest borrowed horses and galloped around the trails. Then they went to Kar-li Caves on the Bhor Ghauts and to Khandala, to the spot where Mr. Young had shot his first tiger.

By the time Florence reboarded the *Deccan*, she felt she understood her father's past a lot better.

The ship sailed on and reached Plymouth, England, in May 1880. Constance was waiting at the dock for them. Florence was thrilled. It had been over three years since Florence had seen her younger sister, and the two of them had a lot of catching up to do.

Florence was not sure how long they would be staying in England, so she made the most of every opportunity to sightsee and visit old friends. She accompanied her father to Edinburgh, where they ordered machinery for the sugar plantation. Then in the autumn Ernest, Florence, and their father went on a tour of France and Italy.

During the summer of 1881, both Florence and her father became ill with typhoid. After a week of raging fever, Florence began a slow recovery. Her father, though, became more ill and dehydrated and died of the disease on October 14, four days after Florence turned twenty-five and he had turned seventy-eight. Florence was well enough to attend the funeral and watch as her father was laid to rest in Cookham Churchyard. She could scarcely believe that both her parents were now gone, and she was thankful for the wonderful times she had had with her father on this trip.

When the funeral was over, the three Young siblings, still grieving their father's sudden death, discussed what to do next. Ernest felt it was time to go to Australia and help with the plantation. Constance was happy and secure in England among her extended family and decided to stay on there. Florence agonized over what she should do. She enjoyed England but could not imagine spending the rest of her life there; she was far too much of a colonial girl for that. But the idea of living on a sugar plantation did not appeal to her either. It was a man's world, and she knew she would be lonely on the plantation. There was one other option. Perhaps she could live in Sydney with Emily and John.

There were eight children in the family now, and Florence was almost certain that Emily would welcome her help.

Florence and Ernest left England in early December 1881. Florence hoped she would find a permanent home with her older sister. She had no idea of the adventures that awaited her in Australia.

Chapter 5

Kanakas

Six months later things were going better than Florence could have imagined. She was now a part of the Deck household in Sydney, where she tutored some of the children and helped Emily with the enormous amount of laundry eleven people produced.

Florence kept in close contact with her brothers through letters. They had finished the house at Fairymead, as they called the plantation, and Ernest began urging Florence to come and visit the place in September 1882. Three days before she was due to leave for Fairymead, one of Emily's friends came to visit. Mrs. Brown was a fellow member of the Plymouth Brethren and an earnest Christian worker. She was well acquainted with the Bundaberg area where the plantation was located. In fact, her husband had once owned the land that was now Fairymead.

Florence, Emily, and Mrs. Brown enjoyed a pleasant visit together. After two hours of conversation, Mrs. Brown announced that it was time for her to go. "Before I leave," she said, "I think we should pray together, don't you?"

Florence and Emily agreed, and the three women knelt to pray. Mrs. Brown prayed first, asking that God would watch over Florence during her visit to Fairymead and make her a blessing to all she met there.

Emily prayed next, and when she finished her prayer Florence began to stand up. As she did so, she felt an arm around her waist. "No, dear, wait a moment," she heard Mrs. Brown say. "You need to pray too."

Florence froze. She had never prayed out loud in front of anyone before. The silence seemed endless as a tug-of-war raged inside Florence. Part of her wanted to pray aloud, but another part of her knew that she would make a fool of herself if she did. Emily and Mrs. Brown waited quietly. Two minutes passed, and then three, before Florence summoned her courage and opened her mouth to speak, but no words came out. She tried again, and this time she managed to say a few words, but she was too nervous to finish her prayer. This time Mrs. Brown squeezed Florence's hand and finished the prayer for her. As the women opened their eyes and stood up, Florence wished she could sink through the floor. She hoped she would never be asked to pray in that way again.

Three days later Florence and her ten-year-old nephew Harry were on their way up the east coast of Australia in a steamer. Florence planned to spend six months in Bundaberg with her brothers before returning to Sydney. It took a week to travel up the coast, and before arriving at Bundaberg, the steamer stopped in the ports of Brisbane and Maryborough. As they traveled north, the weather became increasingly hot and humid.

Fairymead was a five-mile buggy ride from Bundaberg. The road was really a sandy track, and Harry counted five gates that needed to be opened and shut along the way so the buggy could pass. They also had to cross the Burnett River by punt. The buggy ride took two and a half hours, and Florence arrived at the plantation dusty and exhausted. But she was delighted to be once again reunited with her three brothers and see the progress they had made at Fairymead. Everyone was working long days in preparation for the first sugarcane harvest. The juice-extracting machinery that Mr. Young had ordered in Edinburgh before his death had finally arrived and was being assembled. Storage sheds were half built, and there was a vegetable garden that seemed to need constant attention.

Florence found plenty to keep her busy, but she could not seem to forget the words of Mrs. Brown's prayer about being a blessing to all she met. Growing in Florence's heart was the desire to give others the freedom and change she had experience when she became a Christian. But how?

The housekeeper at the plantation lived in a tiny cottage next to the main house. She had four children, and Florence decided they would be her mission field. She gathered the children together and read them Bible stories. Florence even led them in prayers. As she did so, she discovered that she was not nearly as nervous praying in front of children as she had been in front of adults.

Everything was going along well when a realization hit Florence with a force that sent her world spinning. There were eighty indentured laborers living and working at Fairymead. These indentured laborers were known in Australia as Kanakas. They were not native Australians but were natives of the islands of the South Pacific, mainly the New Hebrides and the Solomon Islands. *Eighty people,* Florence told herself, *and not one of them has ever heard of the Christian God. Nor is anyone doing anything to reach them with the gospel message.* It seemed a dreadful state of affairs to Florence, and she could not understand why someone was not doing something about it.

As the days went by, Florence became convinced that if no one else was interested in the Kanaka people, she would have to do something for them herself. Yet the more she learned about the laborers, the more impossible the task seemed. The Kanaka workers spoke many different languages, and the only language they had in common was a smattering of pidgin English—just enough so that their overseers could tell them what to do. In addition, the men came from islands where murder and cannibalism were common, and most of them spent their wages on gambling and drinking. Florence was nervous at the idea of even being in the same room with them. But she fought back her fear and pressed ahead. She asked the head overseer to find out for her whether any of the workers would be interested in a Bible class.

The next Sunday Florence prayed hard as she walked to the old hut where the Bible class was to be held. Her heart was thumping fast as she strolled by a gum tree. There, hanging from a twig, was a chrysalis that sparked an idea. "Thank You, God," she said as she pulled off the twig with the chrysalis on it.

As she neared the hut, Florence counted ten men and a house girl waiting for her. She took a deep breath and stepped inside. "Thank you for coming," she said slowly.

The men stared at her, and Florence realized that this was probably the first time that a white woman had spoken to any of them before. She smiled and held up the chrysalis. "Do you know what's in here?" she asked.

No one spoke.

"A caterpillar made this and got inside it," she continued. "And soon a butterfly will come out. The caterpillar will turn into a butterfly. The Bible tells us that one day, when we die, we will come alive again, and if we know God, we will go to be with Him."

She looked around for any sign of recognition. It was impossible to tell whether or not anyone understood what she had said. Florence decided it was time for a hymn, but none of the Kanakas could read a hymnbook, so instead she sang a chorus and invited the group to sing it line by line after her. This seemed to be more interesting to them than her words about the chrysalis. Florence was amazed at the way they harmonized. When the chorus was finished, she said a prayer, and the meeting was over.

That night Florence thought about how her Bible class had gone. It had not gone very well, she concluded. She doubted that the Kanakas had taken in much of what she said. She knew that it would be so much better if they could read the Bible for themselves. Much to her surprise, Florence found that she did not want to give up trying to reach these people. Instead, her mind whirled with ways to help them. She recalled a set of colored pictures of important Bible stories she had seen in a store in Sydney. She wrote to Emily and asked her to buy the pictures and send them to her as soon as possible. Then Florence tackled the idea of reading. She wanted to teach the Kanakas to read so that they could read the Bible for themselves. Florence did not know whether anyone had ever attempted to teach them to read before, but she was determined to try. She decided to teach them to read directly from the Bible. On a large sheet of paper she wrote out the verse John 3:16: "For God so loved the world that he gave his only begotten son, that whosoever believeth in him should not perish but have everlasting life."

The next Sunday Florence hung the verse on the wall of the hut and pointed to the first word, "God." She said it aloud, and the eleven class members in attendance repeated it after her. Then she moved on to "so" and "loved." Florence spent the rest of the class going over these three words.

That week she went into Bundaberg and purchased twenty large-type New Testaments. She made bookmarks for them all and underlined John 3:16 in red ink. Those in attendance at the Bible class the next Sunday were surprised when she presented each person with a Bible. They all proudly showed each other how they could read some of the words in the underlined verse.

The next Sunday new faces appeared at the Bible class. The students had been busily showing their coworkers the underlined words in the New Testament and how they could pronounce them, and most of the new participants had learned to read the words themselves. It was time to go on to the next verse. As Florence taught more verses to the people, she tried her best to explain their meaning to them. She despaired, though, that the Kanakas would ever understand, because the pidgin English she had taught herself in an attempt to communicate better with them was so limited. So it was a surprise to her when one Sunday Jimmie Aoba, one of the Kanaka laborers who had faithfully attended the Bible class, stayed behind to talk to her.

"What do you want, Jimmie?" Florence asked as she studied his anxious face.

"Missis, me want!"

"What do you want?"

"Me want to *belong* God!" Jimmie replied with great earnestness.

"Wonderful," Florence said. "Keep coming to Bible class and you will learn how to belong God."

But Jimmie shook his head. "Missis, me come along school along Sunday, and then me lose'im six day. Me want to learn quick."

Florence stared at the man in front of her. After all of her hard work, someone was showing an interest in the gospel message. She could hardly believe it.

"You come every night and I teach'im you," Florence replied.

And so Florence began a nightly Bible study with Jimmie and some of his friends. Because they had no permanent meeting place, they met in the washhouse or on the veranda or anywhere else they could find a quiet spot.

Florence was delighted with Jimmie's progress. Jimmie seemed to really understand what he was being taught. Two months later, when he was diagnosed with tuberculosis, his faith did not waiver. He prayed for the other men from his island until the day he died. Although Jimmie's death saddened

Florence, it also made her more determined than ever to keep reaching out to the Kanakas. If Jimmie could understand the message so clearly, she told herself, so could the others.

Florence's brother Horace was planning to marry Ellen Thorne in Sydney at the end of November. The whole Young clan, except for Constance, planned to attend the wedding, and Florence knew that she had a major decision to make before then. Should she return to live with Emily and John, or should she make her home at Fairymead? Eleven months before, as she was planning to leave England for Australia, Florence could never have imagined herself working among the South Sea islanders. But now, as she thought about the decision before her, she realized that her heart was in working among the Kanakas.

Following the wedding in Sydney, Florence collected the rest of her belongings from Emily's house and returned to Fairymead to live. Now that she knew that she was staying long-term, she threw herself into Christian work as never before. She and another Christian woman started giving Bible lessons to the children of settlers at the North Bundaberg state school. Soon Florence opened a branch of the Young People's Scripture Union, with the goal of making God's Good News known to children and youth and encouraging them to seek God through Bible reading and prayer. The branch Florence established soon became the hub for the organization throughout Queensland. Membership in the Young People's Scripture Union quickly grew to four thousand, and Florence was responsible for sending out a monthly newsletter to each member.

Florence's work among the Kanakas was never far from her heart, though it progressed at a more modest pace than the explosive growth of the Young People's Scripture Union. Eighty South Sea islanders were now turning out for her Sunday Bible class, and forty men came each weeknight for reading and religious instruction.

In April 1886 eight converts from the Bible class were baptized, followed in September by nine more baptisms. As she stood listening to the candidates for baptism give their testimonies, Florence was humbled to hear her name spoken many times. She had never imagined being courageous enough to share her faith with others. But she had overcome her fear, and now she was seeing her efforts rewarded.

Early in 1886 Florence had begun to think about the other plantations in the area. She found out that about three thousand Kanakas were working within thirty miles of Fairymead, with about ten thousand altogether in Queensland. The more Florence thought and prayed, the more convinced she became that each plantation needed its own "missionary" to the Kanakas. But when she told her friends about her plan, they all tried to discourage her. "Planters would not allow such classes," they said. "And where would you get the money to support these workers, anyway?"

Florence would not give up, and she was very excited when she learned that a Christian worker named Ella Dowling was coming to spend the winter at Fairymead. Ella, a friend of Emily's, had been sick for the past five years. Even in her weakened state, twenty-two-year-old Ella had organized a mission in Victoria, and Florence hoped that she would help with evangelizing the Kanakas in Queensland.

Florence and Ella liked each other immediately, and they often prayed together about the need for workers to extend the work to the Kanakas. They decided to name their work the Queensland Kanaka Mission. Ella helped Florence write a circular letter laying out the urgent needs of the new organization. The women sent copies of the letter to Christians they knew in Australia and overseas.

A month after sending out the circular letter, Florence received a letter from her sister Emily. Inside the envelope were two neatly folded one-guinea notes. Florence began to read the letter that accompanied them. In it Emily told how she had gone to a meeting to hear George Müller preach. Müller ran a large orphanage in Bristol, England, and he was visiting Australia and New Zealand on a speaking tour. Emily wrote: "After the meeting I introduced myself and showed Mr. Müller your letter. He read it in a slow quiet way, and then he said, 'I think the Lord wants me to help this work.' Florence, isn't that wonderful? He gave me two guineas, and then do you know what he said? 'Tell your sister to expect *great things* from God, and she will get them.'"

Tears came to Florence's eyes as she read the words. She and Ella were indeed believing for great things—another worker, more New Testaments, more paper and pencils.

While George Müller was the first to contribute to the Queensland Kanaka Mission, others quickly followed. Soon there was enough money to support a worker for three months, although there were no workers in sight yet. To make matters worse, Ella's health had deteriorated still further, and in August 1886 she died. Heartbroken by the loss, Florence did her best to continue to expect great things from God, but it was difficult for her to see how things would work out.

Chapter 6

"Why Don't You Go?"

On a particularly hot day in January 1887, Florence Young stood at the door of a modest cottage. Her brother Ernest had just rented it, and she was preparing the place for the arrival of Carl Johnston and his wife. The Johnstons were a Swedish couple who had been missionaries in the Congo in Africa. They had received a copy of Florence's letter and had contacted her to offer their services to the new mission. Florence was delighted. The Johnstons sounded like just the kind of workers she and Ella had prayed for, and she eagerly anticipated their arrival.

With more workers, the plan was for the Kanakas to gather on Sunday in the mission hall, which Ernest had also donated. Carl Johnston would hold a service there for the men. Each weeknight Carl would then ride out to a different plantation to teach and preach to the local Kanakas.

After the Johnstons' arrival, things got off to a slow start. The Kanakas seemed to find it easier to learn from a woman, and Florence found herself having to spend many evenings encouraging Carl to continue with the work.

Eventually things began to improve. In August seventeen more converts from other plantations were baptized. Then in October another missionary couple, Arthur Eustace and his wife, arrived from Victoria, Australia, to work with Queensland Kanaka Mission. With their arrival, Florence divided up the territory. The Eustaces worked in the Woongarra district to the south while the Johnstons concentrated their efforts on the north side of the nearby Auburn River.

The mission now had five workers and was starting to make an impact, not only on the Kanakas but also on their employers. For the mission to be allowed onto the various plantations, Florence had made a promise that she would never ask the planters for money. So she was surprised when Bill Williamson approached her after Bible class at a neighboring plantation. Bill had been doubtful about letting his Kanaka workers take Bible lessons. Now he looked sheepish.

"When you started this work, Miss Young," Bill began, "I told you I did not believe you would see any results. But I can't help seeing them myself.

Some of the worst and most troublesome boys on the plantation have been completely changed."

"I'm glad to hear that," Florence replied. It was not often that a plantation owner offered such praise.

Bill continued. "You said you would not ask for money."

Florence nodded. "No, and I never will."

"But it is worth money to me. My boys do better work, and I think we planters ought to contribute to the cost of the mission."

"Oh, yes," Florence said, "I think so too, but I promised never to ask for your help."

"I want to give it anyway. I have decided to give a donation each month on behalf of my boys." With that, Bill drew some banknotes from his pocket. "This is a start. You can expect more on the first of the month."

Florence was delighted, not just because the money would help out with the mission's expenses but because it showed that the Kanaka converts were changed people.

Over time the system of "bringing one friend" developed. Florence and the other Queensland Kanaka Mission workers found that it was very effective to have their converts target one friend at a time to bring to Christ. They urged the convert to pray for their friend and invite him to Bible class until he, too, was converted.

This approach appealed to the Kanakas, even though some of them still found it a challenge. One of these converts was Caleb, a lovable but not very persuasive Christian. Caleb decided to pray for his friend Tara-vega, but no matter what he did, he could not get his friend to come along to the Bible class with him.

Florence encouraged Caleb not to give up. "Well, Caleb," she told him, "I think very good you pray first time; then you ask him Tara-vega. I think he come."

The next evening Caleb arrived with Tara-vega beside him. Tara-vega sat quietly through the class, and afterward Caleb brought him to Florence to have his name registered as a student.

"Me buy'im that one along school, Missis," Caleb said, puffing out his chest.

"You do what?" Florence asked, although she was quite sure of what she had heard.

"Me buy'im along school. Me ask'im all the time come along school; he no want'im; he no like school. So me tell him, 'Suppose you come along school one month. You come every night, you no stop away one night, me give you sixpence!'"

Caleb looked so proud of his "witnessing scheme" that Florence tried to look serious. Then he added, "He no like'im school. By and by he like'im plenty; he come all the time."

Tara-vega did come to class every night for a month, at the end of which time he was beginning to read and understand the gospel message. After he collected his sixpence from Caleb, he kept coming and was soon converted.

In April 1888 Florence received a letter that changed her immediate plans. The letter was from a

Mrs. Smith of County Limerick, Ireland. Florence's sister Constance had been engaged to Mrs. Smith's son Willoughby, but sadly, he had died of pneumonia before the wedding. Constance had gone to stay with Willoughby's family, but she was not doing well. Mrs. Smith wrote that Constance was so upset that she hardly ate. She asked if someone from the family would come and get her right away and take her back to Australia, where perhaps a change of scenery would help her forget Willoughby.

Florence made arrangements to leave right away. She asked her sister-in-law Ellen to cover the mission work at Fairymead, and within a week she was on her way to Ireland.

When Florence finally arrived in Ireland, Constance was feeling a little stronger and insisted that she did not want to go back to Australia. She felt she belonged in Ireland. She had her heart set on buying a small home in the country, where she planned to invite poor children from Dublin to stay with her for a week or two at a time. Florence understood her younger sister's desire to do something worthwhile. Instead of insisting that she return to Australia, she helped Constance settle into a home near Bagnalstown, not far from Dublin.

Before returning to Australia, Florence accompanied her cousin William Mackworth Young and his wife to Rawalpindi, India, where her cousin had just been appointed commissioner. She spent three weeks in Rawalpindi before setting out on a tour of India. Her first stop was Peshawar, located on India's border with Afghanistan. Florence stayed in this isolated city with three English women who were missionaries. In fact, the women were the only three British residents in the place, and Florence was impressed by their courage as they lived in this remote city surrounded by so many ardent Muslims.

From Peshawar, Florence traveled by train across India to Calcutta, stopping at Agra, Delhi, and Benares along the way. From Calcutta she made her way to Darjeeling for a few days of relaxation in the foothills of the Himalayan Mountains. From there she traveled on to Colombo, Ceylon (later renamed Sri Lanka), where she had an eleven-day wait for the arrival of the steamer that would carry her to Australia.

Florence arrived back at Fairymead in May 1889, relieved to find that things had gone well in her absence and that the Queensland Kanaka Mission was thriving. While she was away, the Kanakas had been the focus of a government investigation. It turned out that many of the Kanakas had been lured on board ships and taken to the coast of Australia against their will. Others had agreed to come to Australia, but it was doubtful whether they had any understanding of the fact that they would have to endure three years of hard labor upon their arrival. The results of the investigation shocked Florence, who was glad to hear that legislation had been introduced into parliament to end this practice of "blackbirding," or tricking Kanakas into leaving their home islands. The legislation would stop any further blackbirding, and those Kanakas already in

Queensland were advised to complete their three-year work terms and then return home.

The new focus of the Queensland Kanaka Mission was to reach every possible Kanaka man before he returned to his island, and Florence redoubled her efforts to convert and train the young men.

In February 1890 Florence learned that one of her heroes, the famous missionary Hudson Taylor, of the China Inland Mission, was visiting Australia. Florence desperately wanted to hear him speak, so she attended a conference in Brisbane where he was scheduled to preach. Regrettably, the steamer carrying Taylor ran aground on a sandbank near Rockhampton, farther down the coast, delaying his appearance at the conference. Florence was disappointed. She assumed that she had missed her opportunity to hear Taylor, but much to her surprise, right in the middle of one of the conference meetings, the preacher brought a stranger up onto the platform.

The stranger was a short man, rather shabbily dressed in a dusty coat. *Surely,* Florence thought, *this cannot be the great Hudson Taylor everyone talks about.* But it was, and with a single sentence of introduction, Taylor launched into a sermon that was to change Florence's life. As Taylor spoke of the millions of unreached people in China, a thought flashed through Florence's mind. *This is dreadful. Why don't Christians go to them?* Instantly she heard a voice in her head: *Why don't you go?*

Me! Florence countered. *I could never leave my Kanaka boys.*

As Hudson Taylor preached on, Florence tried to get the notion of going to China out of her head, but it would not budge.

If I want you in China, she felt God say to her, *do you think you will be any use in Queensland?*

Florence surrendered. *Lord, I'm Yours,* she said. *If You want me to go to China, I am prepared to leave my work here and go.*

The following day Florence spoke privately with Hudson Taylor. She explained to him about the work of the Queensland Kanaka Mission and told him that she felt called to work in China.

"You must be very sure it is God's leading, since you are doing such a fruitful work in Queensland," he cautioned. "You would be faced with many new trials in China. But if God does send you, we will give you a warm welcome."

The following day Florence received a sad telegram from Fairymead. Her sister Constance had died in Ireland of heart failure at the age of thirty-two. Florence was glad to be in the company of so many Christians who could pray for and encourage her and help her through her grief.

When Florence got back to Fairymead, she could not shake the idea that she was supposed to go to China with the China Inland Mission (CIM). With no more Kanakas coming to Queensland and the numbers of those working on the plantations diminishing, Florence conceded that it was possible for her to leave the ongoing work in the hands of her sister-in-law Ellen.

"Why Don't You Go?"

By January 1891 Florence was convinced that her future lay in China. She sent off an application to the CIM office in Sydney and waited eagerly for a response. A group of new missionaries was due to leave in March for China, and Florence hoped to be a part of the group.

Through each passing week, Florence waited eagerly for the mail to arrive. But she received no news from the China Inland Mission. March came, and still there was no news.

During March Florence traveled to Sydney to attend the marriage of her brother Ernest to Margaret Adam. While there, she had the opportunity to attend the farewell service for the CIM missionaries heading to China. When the service was over, she asked the leader of the mission why she had heard nothing from the CIM council. Much to Florence's dismay, she learned that her application had never reached the office in Sydney. Before she left to return home, she filled out another application and handed it in personally.

Within days word came back that Florence had been accepted for the work in China. The China Inland Mission gave her six weeks to wind up her affairs and be ready to depart.

Florence was kept busy during this time packing, saying good-bye to her family and friends, and handing over leadership of the Queensland Kanaka Mission to Ellen.

Finally May 26, 1891, arrived, and Florence Young stood at the railing of the SS *Airlie*, watching as the city of Brisbane faded from view. She felt like Abraham in the Old Testament, leaving everything she knew behind her.

Chapter 7

China

The SS *Airlie* reached the port of Hong Kong on the afternoon of June 18, 1891. Florence peered over the railing at the junks and houseboats that quickly surrounded the ship. As soon as they dropped anchor, the noise on board rose to a crescendo as Chinese men scrambled aboard shouting and screaming at the passengers. Florence's heart dropped. Were these the people she had come to serve? They acted nothing like Australians, or Pacific islanders, for that matter. She began to wonder whether she could ever relate to them. Had she made a terrible mistake?

Just before dinner Florence and several other passengers went ashore and walked around the dock area, and Florence found herself again asking the same question. This time the question arose as a result of what she read in an English-language newspaper. The paper carried a lurid report of a riot in Wu-Su, China, recounting how a mob had attacked a mission compound. The women and children at the compound had escaped in their pajamas, but the two male missionaries had been murdered. The article went on to conclude that war between China and the foreign powers that occupied many of her port cities was imminent and that all Europeans should leave China immediately.

Florence imagined Hudson Taylor in Shanghai offering refuge to the four hundred or so China Inland Mission missionaries who would be forced to evacuate the inland areas. That night she wrote to Emily, trying to describe her feelings:

> To-day's paper is full of the serious riots in various places, and of the possibility of further troubles. It has been rather a testing time for me. Do you remember our walk at Wooloomooloo, when I told you how easily frightened I am? Well, I am a coward, and I confess my heart and my flesh have felt very much like shrinking from what might lie in store for us. Only "God is the strength of my heart, and my portion for ever."

The following day Captain Ellis took Florence and two other women sightseeing around Hong Kong. Florence was intrigued by Hong Kong Island.

It was densely populated, and the narrow streets were barely wide enough for rickshaws to pass along. The island was dominated by Victoria Peak, which rose to a height of 1,825 feet. On the lower slopes of the peak was the European quarter, tucked behind the markets and commercial center of Hong Kong that occupied the narrow strip of flat land between the base of the peak and the sea. Captain Ellis walked the women through the quarter on tree-lined streets, along which sat bungalows with neat English gardens.

They rode to the top of Victoria Peak on a cable car. Florence drank in the magnificent view from the summit. Ships bobbed on the harbor's azure water like toy boats. Beyond lay Kowloon peninsula, and beyond that the mainland of China itself. Florence noted that the air at the top of the peak was much cooler and crisper than the stifling, humid atmosphere of the city below.

Florence was to transfer to a steamer in Hong Kong that would take her on to Shanghai. Captain Ellis kindly allowed her to stay on the *Airlie* until the steamer for Shanghai was ready for her to board. The following day the *Airlie* was to take on coal for its onward journey. Florence and another woman and her five small children, who were to catch a steamer on to Japan, went ashore for the day, where they went by rickshaw to visit "Happy Valley," supposedly one of the most beautiful cemeteries in the world. By the time Florence arrived at the cemetery, she was feeling chilled and her hands were shaking. She did not improve as the day went on, and when she returned to the ship, Captain Ellis was very concerned about her. He checked in on Florence first thing in the morning, and when he found her no better, he summoned a doctor.

Dr. Thompson examined Florence and pronounced that she had Hong Kong fever and could not travel any farther until she was better. Regrettably, the SS *Airlie* would be leaving port in the next day or two, leaving Florence with nowhere to go to recover.

The problem was solved when Dr. Thompson invited Florence to stay at a missionary sanatorium on Victoria Peak. The doctor agreed to make the necessary arrangements and gave Florence some quinine to bring her fever down. Later that day Captain Ellis accompanied Florence to the sanatorium. Florence was groggy and barely remembered the trip there.

For the first few days, Florence hardly knew where she was. She looked out the sanatorium window occasionally, but all she could see was a thick fog. Every joint and muscle in her body ached, and she hated to think that this was her missionary debut.

Florence remained under Dr. Thompson's care for eight days before he pronounced her strong enough to continue her journey to Shanghai. He warned Florence that she would suffer relapses of the fever and gave her some more medicines to take whenever she did so.

Florence had no adequate words to thank the doctor when she left. He had cared for her, a complete stranger, and probably saved her life.

Finally, on July 3, 1891, Florence Young arrived at the China Inland Mission home in Shanghai. Hudson Taylor and his wife greeted her warmly and made sure that she had everything she needed. Florence was grateful to learn that the local disturbances against foreigners had died down during the time she had been ill and that the work of the mission inland continued.

Florence suffered a relapse of Hong Kong fever while she was at the mission home, and it was twelve days before she could travel on to the language training school located at Yang-chau.

The day before she was due to travel, Hudson Taylor's wife presented Florence with an outfit of women's clothing. Florence already knew that Hudson Taylor had very definite views about how a missionary should present him or herself, and this included dressing like the local people. It had shocked the English establishment when Taylor first grew his hair long and wore it in a queue—a single braid down his back. But over the years his policy had proved wise.

Now it was time for Florence to don a long dress, covered by a tunic with wide sleeves, and put on embroidered cloth shoes. She was surprised at how comfortable the clothing was and how much less attention she attracted to herself wearing it. In fact, with her black hair slicked back into a bun,

Florence imagined that from behind she looked just like any other Chinese woman.

Florence was still feeling sickly when she left for Yang-chau. Five other missionary recruits were journeying with her, and a seasoned missionary named John McCarthy acted as their escort. The first leg of the journey was a two-hundred-mile voyage up the Yangtze River to the treaty port of Chin-kiang. Because the missionaries were dressed in native garb rather than in European clothing, the steamship owner allowed them to travel steerage with the Chinese passengers, paying a fare of half a dollar instead of the twenty dollars for an above-deck cabin. The food, when Florence had the strength to eat it, was excellent. The steamer supplied hot rice, boiling water for tea, and chopsticks. For a few pennies, one of the stewards produced vegetables and seafood to accompany the rice.

Florence was amazed at how muddy the water became as the ship steamed upriver. It reminded her of pea soup, and she understood why Hudson Taylor had warned her to make sure all of her drinking water was boiled first.

It took two days to reach Chin-kiang, where John hired a riverboat to cross the Yangtze River and head up the Grand Canal. Finally the riverboat deposited the group on the side of the Grand Canal, from where it was a twenty-minute wheelbarrow ride to Yang-chau.

Florence had never experienced anything like her first wheelbarrow ride, and she never wanted to repeat it. In relating the story of the ride she wrote to Emily:

> They are simply instruments of torture. There is a big wooden wheel in the center, protected by a framework. On each side of the wheel is a shelf of wooden bars upon which you sit. With one arm you cling to the center frame and with the other you try to keep an umbrella over your head, a difficult matter in the crowded narrow alleys. And words will not describe the bumping. The alleys, I can't call them streets, are paved with lumps of stone, you go bump, bump, bump all the way. After two or three minutes you are thankful to get off and walk a few steps to relieve your back; but not having a Chinese woman with us, this was not proper.

The grueling trip ended at Yang-chau, the location of the China Inland Mission's women's language school. Here Florence would embark upon six months of intensive study of the Mandarin language.

Life soon fell into a routine at the school. John McCarthy's sister was the housekeeper, and she awoke the students at 5:30 each morning with a cup of tea. Then it was breakfast, followed by one hour of personal prayer and Bible study. After prayer and Bible study came six hours of language study. Most of the other women in the school were enthusiastic about their future, but Florence found herself dreading what lay ahead. In her journal she let out her feelings:

> The other women here say they have never felt the Lord so near. To me He has never seemed so far away. They speak of the *dear* Chinese, of how their hearts go out to them. I think they are dreadful. Perhaps the sickness and drugs have drained every bit of buoyancy out of me, but I am in a dark, dark valley of humiliation. I am so bitterly disappointed. I did so want to give the Lord a glad and joyful offering.

Gradually, though, Florence began to adjust to life in China and her Mandarin studies. The language was more difficult than she had imagined, and her studies were interrupted when she was asked to go to Chin-kiang for five weeks to nurse a missionary who had rheumatic fever.

Finally, in February 1892, Florence was assigned to her first missionary posting at Kiu-kiang, in Kiang-si province to the west. This was a well-established mission station staffed by two single women missionaries, a Chinese Bible teacher and her son, and a young evangelist and his wife.

Again, the journey to Kiu-kiang involved a boat trip, this time across P'oyang Lake and up the Kuangsin River. In all, eleven women graduates of the language school, including seven Swedes, set out on the journey with a male missionary escort.

The women would be dropped at various mission stations along the way.

When Florence arrived at Kiu-kiang, she found the local dialect almost impossible to understand. On the first Sunday there, Florence was asked by one of the other missionaries to give her testimony during the morning service. Florence had never done this in English, much less Chinese. However, in her eight months with the China Inland Mission, she had learned one thing—you should give yourself to every opportunity, even if you feel you cannot do it well.

After Florence had said a few introductory words, several people in the front row snickered. Within a minute just about all the Chinese people in attendance were laughing loudly. Florence made a couple more attempts and then sat down. She had never felt so humiliated in her life, and by the people she was supposed to love and serve.

When the meeting was over, the local Bible teacher, Mrs. Hong, patted Florence on the hand. "It will be all right. Let your heart rest," she said. "If you eat our rice, you will soon speak our words."

Much to Florence's relief, Mrs. Hong proved to be correct. Now that she was spending almost all her time with Chinese people, Florence found her Mandarin improving each day. She also began to accept and even enjoy the Chinese way of doing things.

Florence had not been in Kiu-kiang long when Mrs. Hong invited her to visit a village about nine miles away. Instead of dreading the bone-shaking wheelbarrow ride, Florence had by now learned to balance on the barrow perfectly, and she could sit on it happily for hours at a time.

Mrs. Hong was an elderly woman who was nearly blind, and they traveled slowly for her sake. They arrived in the village in midafternoon and were immediately invited into a convert's home for a meal. The walls of the house were made of dried mud over which had been stretched a tile roof. The roof tiles were black from the smoke of the fire in the kitchen. On the other side of the room from the kitchen was a pigsty that housed a sow and several squealing piglets. Florence and Mrs. Hong sat on the uneven earthen floor between the kitchen and the pigsty, and the meal was spread before them. The whole family gathered round as they ate rice, stewed melon, and salted vegetables. Anything that was not eaten by the humans was scooped up by the scavenging chickens that scooted in and out of the house. Florence smiled as she ate, thinking of how different this was from eating with her aunts in England with maids and butlers in attendance.

That night Florence and Mrs. Hong slept on an old bedstead whose metal frame had been piled with fresh straw for a mattress. Florence was surprised at the good night's sleep she had on the old bedstead.

Florence continued to visit outlying villages and learn more of the local language until May 1893, when the mission superintendent for the area, Mr. Orr-Ewing, asked her to take charge of the mission's work at Ho-k'eo. Miss Gibson, the missionary who headed up the work there, consisting of a large church with four outstations, was taking a year's furlough.

Florence's heart sank when she heard the news. Miss Gibson was the best Mandarin speaker in the province, and she knew all of the local customs and ways of getting things done. Florence, on the other hand, was still struggling with the language and was constantly making awkward mistakes in front of Chinese people. Still, she packed up her few belongings and set out on the two-day barrow ride to her new home in Ho-k'eo.

Florence's new home was not nearly as comfortable as her previous one. A flood had swept through the house two weeks before, and everything was damp and moldering. Florence did her best to continue the work Miss Gibson had done, but it was difficult, especially when she got malaria and had to be nursed by the Chinese workers.

Although very challenging, the twelve months at Ho-k'eo helped Florence gain confidence in the culture and language, and when Miss Gibson arrived back, Mr. Orr-Ewing suggested that Florence open up a new mission station in nearby Ien-shan. A large house was secured at Ien-shan, and Florence and several other women missionaries moved in. The house was soon inundated with curious local people who came to see what Christians were like. The locals did not knock; they just walked into the house. Sometimes there were as many as twenty people wandering around the house, checking what was in the trunks, watching Florence bake scones in a kerosene tin oven, or asking questions about the Christian faith.

One such person who came to check out the house was a man named Liao. He was an opium addict and asked Florence if she had medicines to cure him of his addiction. Florence explained that she did not but that Jesus Christ could change his life and help him overcome his addiction. After several visits Liao decided to become a Christian and asked God to help him overcome his addiction. It was not easy for him, and when he craved opium, he would visit the mission house, where the missionaries would pray for and with him. Slowly, over several weeks, Liao broke his addiction to opium. Florence was amazed at the change in Liao's appearance. Now he held his shoulders back and his head high, and his face beamed with new life and vitality. Soon he began traveling to outlying villages, where he would tell people, "Yes, indeed, this Savior is a great Savior. He saved me from my opium." Then Liao would point at his face and add, "Look at me. Am I not Hao-k'an, beautiful to behold."

The work at Ien-shan was exhausting for Florence, especially when her malaria recurred. As the year progressed, Florence received letters from Australia, bearing the news that her oldest niece, Kathleen Deck, had gone to Fairymead to work with the Queensland Kanaka Mission. Florence's sister-in-law Ellen, however, was finding it increasingly difficult to keep going with the work of the mission. When Florence had left Australia in 1891, the government had just passed an act ending the importation of Kanaka labor in three years. But under pressure from the sugarcane growers, the government had reversed itself and revoked the act. Now the Kanakas were a permanent part of the Queensland labor force.

This news tore Florence in two. After three years of learning the language, she was becoming quite fluent in Mandarin and felt she was now of some real use to the China Inland Mission. On the other hand, she could not get the needs of the Queensland Kanaka Mission out of her thoughts. She prayed that God would show her very clearly whether she should stay in China or go home and sort out the problems with the mission in Queensland. Florence was not prepared for the speed or the decisiveness of the answer to her prayer for guidance.

Chapter 8

"Not in Vain"

That following Sunday, Florence had a particularly busy day of preaching and praying with people. Things were finally winding down in the evening when a messenger told her that the landlord wanted to see her immediately. According to the messenger, the landlord was hiding in her kitchen.

As Florence crossed the courtyard to the house, she thought about how odd this was. The landlord lived about ten miles away in another village, and he never traveled at night. And why, she wondered, was he hiding in the kitchen?

When Florence opened the kitchen door she spotted her landlord sitting on a stool in the shadows. His hands were shaking, and he looked like he had seen a ghost.

"What is it?" Florence asked, walking over to him.

He held his finger to his lips. "Speak quietly," he said.

"Well?" Florence whispered.

"It is the mandarin," he replied. "He always boasted that he would never allow a Christian church at Ien-shan, and now he is making good on his word. Tonight he ordered soldiers to come to my house and beat me until I threw you out of this place, but someone warned me and I fled."

Florence's mind was whirling. She scarcely knew what to think. She was aware that the mandarin did not want Christians in his city, but she had been here for three months now and he had never protested her presence.

"Why is he doing this now?" she asked.

"His wife has been very ill this last year, and he has been watching over her. But she died yesterday morning, and now he has made it his mission to purge the city of you."

"Lord help us," Florence said. "We are no match for the power of a mandarin unless we have God's help."

"God's help or not, you have to hide me somewhere or I will be killed," the landlord replied.

"I suppose you can stay in the cellar," Florence said. "It won't be very comfortable, but you can't see it from the road, and you should be safe there. In the meantime I will write to Miss Gibson and ask her to help us. She understands much more about these things than I do."

Later that night Florence sat in her bedroom writing to Miss Gibson, begging her to come to Ien-shan as soon as the messenger gave her the letter.

After the messenger left with the letter, it was a matter of waiting to see what the mandarin would do next. Florence did not have to wait long to find out. On Tuesday he tried to get the local people to riot against Florence and burn down her house. When some Christian men came to the mission's rescue, a nasty confrontation took place, and Florence was grateful that no one was killed. A week later the mandarin threatened the city rulers with a thousand blows each if they did not lay charges against Florence, and then he arrested the landlord's wife.

In the midst of this, Miss Gibson arrived with a native evangelist from Ho-k'eo. Despite their understanding of local ways, neither of them could get the mandarin to listen to reason. Eventually Miss Gibson told Florence that the only way to get the landlord's wife released from prison was to promise that they would all leave Ien-shan the following day. Less than three weeks after Florence had prayed to be shown whether she should stay or go, she was hurriedly packing her bags to leave.

Florence decided to travel to Shanghai to meet with Hudson Taylor. Another Australian missionary, Anne Bavin, accompanied her to the coast. When she arrived in Shanghai, Florence showed Hudson the letters pleading for her to go home to help the Queensland Kanaka Mission.

Two days later Hudson called Florence into his office. He handed the letters back to her. "I believe it is God's will for you to go home," he said.

"Do you think I should come back?" Florence asked.

"I cannot say, only put yourself at the Lord's disposal, and He will guide you."

While she stayed in the CIM guest house in Shanghai, Florence learned news of what was happening in the world. In June 1894 Chinese and Japanese troops had both landed in Korea. The Chinese had dominated the Korean peninsula since the seventeenth century, and now the Japanese wanted to take it over. The Japanese seemed to have the upper hand, and antiforeign hostilities were building again in China. Over her time in China, Florence had grown attached to the Chinese people, and she hated to think of leaving the country at such a needy time, but Hudson Taylor had told her he felt it was right that she should go.

It was not until Florence was aboard the SS *Airlie*, the same vessel that had brought her to China, that she realized just how exhausted she was. Florence enjoyed quiet talks with Captain Ellis, who was once again in command of the ship, and Bible studies with Anne Bavin, who was returning to Australia on the same vessel. Florence celebrated her thirty-eighth birthday quietly as the *Airlie* steamed down the east coast of Australia.

In Brisbane, Florence disembarked and was greeted by her sister Emily and various nieces and nephews. She marveled at how much the younger children had grown in the three years she had been away. From Brisbane Florence went straight back to Fairymead to see her brothers and their growing families.

When she had caught up with all of her family members, Florence turned her attention to the Queensland Kanaka Mission. Now that there was no end in sight to the flow of Kanaka workers coming into Australia, Florence paid more attention to the way the mission was organized. She appointed a Council of Advice to help run the organization and worked hard at attracting more missionaries to come and work in Queensland.

Although it was a difficult task, Florence was determined to see the mission flourish, and in January 1895 a middle-aged couple and another single woman came to join the work. This freed Florence up for the one thing she needed more than anything else—rest.

Emily arranged for her, Florence, Anne Bavin, and Horace to visit New Zealand. Their first port of call was Stewart Island, the southernmost island of New Zealand. Emily's son Samuel and his wife had set up a farm there, and it was just the place Florence needed to be.

It was a glorious summer, and Samuel took the party out on his yacht. As they explored the wild, deserted coves and bays of the island, Florence began to relax for the first time in years. She wandered along paths through the dense forest, stopping to admire the native tree ferns, or pungas, as the Maoris called them. The damp, quiet forests and memories of her childhood at Erme Dale soothed Florence's nerves.

One week went by, and then another, until a whole month had passed before Florence and Anne felt ready to continue their travels, accompanied by Emily and Horace. Their plan was to hold missionary meetings in various towns at the southern end of South Island. It was a discouraging task, as minister after minister told them that there was no interest in missions at the moment. Florence went right ahead with the meetings anyway.

Their first stop was Invercargill, where a small hall was available. The hall seated three hundred people, which the local minister told them was many more people than they could realistically expect to attract. Emily, though, had other ideas. She asked if something bigger was available and was told about the town theater, which seated fifteen hundred people and cost four guineas a night to hire.

"Engage the theater," Emily instructed. "Advertise free seats and no collection, and then we'll start praying."

And pray they did. On the night of the meeting, Florence and Anne walked to the theater. As they entered it, they were shocked. The place was packed to the doors. There wasn't even any more standing room.

Florence gasped. "There must be two thousand people packed in here. What are we going to do,

Anne? How are we supposed to talk to all these people? I have never talked to this many people in my life. I don't think I can do it."

"Nor do I," Anne replied shakily. "I had no idea it would be like this."

Just then Emily walked up behind them. "Come on," she encouraged them. "We prayed that God would create an interest in missions in Invercargill, and He has. We need to be grateful, not afraid that so many people have turned up. When you open your mouth, God will give you the words to speak. Come on, let's get you both dressed in your Chinese attire."

Florence nodded. Of course this was a wonderful opportunity, and her sister was right. It would be a sin not to use it to its fullest advantage.

Anne spoke first, telling about the life of a missionary in China, the obstacles of daily living, including the complex language, and the antiforeign sentiments. Then it was Florence's turn to speak. She spoke on the history of the China Inland Mission and the life of Hudson Taylor. When the meeting was over, the audience clapped for the two women and rose to their feet. Florence was delighted to hear that there were many new faces at Invercargill churches on Sunday and that many people wanted to learn more about how to support missionaries.

Their next meeting was at Winton. The Presbyterian minister there had helped to arrange things for the duo, including providing the hall for the meeting. When Florence and Anne arrived in town, the minister's wife tried to prepare them for the small audiences she expected would turn up.

"I hate to say this," she said, "but our people never come out to missionary meetings, and it has been very short notice. The country people don't even know it's on."

That afternoon Florence, Horace, and Emily walked around to look at the hall. The janitor let them in. The hall had a platform with a row of ten chairs facing it.

"Where are the rest of the seats?" Emily asked.

"Oh," the janitor replied, "there's plenty here. But you won't want any more."

"But where are they?" Emily persisted.

"Under the platform," the janitor said.

"Well, get them out," Florence heard her sister say. "Every one of them."

The janitor muttered something about silly women, but he got down on his hands and knees and started pulling folding chairs out from under the platform. Dust flew everywhere.

"Make sure they are all cleaned and set out," Emily said. "We've paid for the hall already, and that includes seating."

"All right," the man said. "Everything will be done by tonight. Though I don't know what for."

That night Florence and the others walked back to the hall. The Presbyterian minister's wife came with them. Florence saw two women entering the hall and heard the minister's wife give a sigh of relief. "At least *someone* will be there," she said.

But a surprise awaited them inside. For a second time in a week, a hall was filled to overflowing with people wanting to hear Florence and Anne speak. The crowd sat in silence as Anne and then Florence talked about their lives as missionaries in China.

These two meetings set the tone for the rest of the missionary tour, in which the two women spoke to over seventy meetings during the next three months.

Despite the heavy schedule, Florence returned to Fairymead feeling rested and ready to help with the work of the Queensland Kanaka Mission. By now the mission had five workers. Florence's niece Kathleen worked at Fairymead, Arthur Eustace and his wife were at the Kalkie plantation, and James McKenzie and his wife worked in North Bundaberg.

The work was helped along by the visit of William Lindsay in 1896. William was the editor of the China Inland Missions newsletter, and he stopped in to see how Florence's work was going. While he was there, he helped her to write a newsletter for the Queensland Kanaka Mission. Florence did not know what to call the newsletter until she attended a funeral for one of the Kanaka men.

The man's name was David, and he came from the island of Aoba. While Florence had been in New Zealand, David had become so ill that the overseer recommended he be sent home to die. He was put on a ship at Bundaberg, but the vessel sailed into a hurricane. As ill as he was, David gathered the other Kanaka passengers on board and prayed for everyone's safety. The hurricane passed, but the ship was damaged and had to return to Bundaberg. By now, David had changed his mind about going back to the islands. "Me like to be planted along Fairymead," he said. So Kathleen Deck had taken him in and nursed him until he died.

At the funeral Kathleen told how David looked forward to being with Jesus. He often said, "By-and-by me see Jesus, me thank Him plenty."

Then as Florence and the small group gathered around the open grave, James McKenzie read the verse, "Therefore, my beloved brethren, be ye stedfast, unmoveable, always abounding in the work of the Lord, forasmuch as ye know that your labour is not in vain in the Lord" (1 Cor. 15:58).

The words "not in vain" echoed in Florence's mind. She decided the phrase should be the name of the mission's new newsletter.

Later in the year, Florence gathered in the North Bundaberg Hall with two hundred Kanaka men. The service was like any other Sunday morning service. The worshipers sang several hymns, and some of the men prayed aloud before the preacher stood to deliver the morning message. After the message, they all ate lunch together, and then the service reconvened on the bank of a nearby river. Florence's heart throbbed with delight. One hundred fifteen Kanaka men were about to be baptized. As the last bars of the hymn "I'm Not Ashamed to Own My Lord" died away, one man after the other filed into the clear water of the river to be baptized. It was a joyous day for all involved in the Queensland Kanaka Mission.

Following the baptismal service, Florence marveled at how things were going. The mission was functioning well, and they were seeing results. Florence had accomplished what she had set out to do, and she began to wonder what she should do next.

Chapter 9

An-ren

By 1897 Florence felt the now familiar pull in two directions. To the sadness of Florence and the whole Queensland Kanaka Mission, James McKenzie had drowned, and though still committed to the mission, Kathleen Deck had endured a physical breakdown. Still, the work among the Kanakas was going well, and Walter Fricke, a new worker, was appointed superintendent under the direction of Florence's brother Ernest and the Council of Advice. At the same time, Florence kept in touch with many of the China Inland Mission missionaries and learned that the need for workers in China was greater than ever.

After much soul searching, Florence decided that she should return to China. She left Sydney just after her forty-first birthday in October 1897. When

Florence arrived in China, she was appointed to lead the eight-year-old mission station at An-ren, the first in a chain of mission stations on the Kuang-sin River. The mission station consisted of forty-eight church members and two outstations.

Two other single women missionaries, Christine Muldoon and Emma Forsberg, greeted Florence when she finally arrived at An-ren. At first Florence felt very out of place. She had been away from China for three years and in that time had forgotten much of her Mandarin. Not that it mattered, she realized. The local people spoke such a strange variation of Mandarin that she barely understood a word of what they said. Even the Chinese evangelist, Iao, who came from another district, was often misunderstood, and he had been living in An-ren for the entire eight years the mission station had been there. All of this was discouraging to Florence, but she tried as hard as she could and prayed that God would help the people to understand her.

Once in An-ren Florence seldom had a quiet moment. A busy street edged right up to the mission house, and shouting and bartering took place outside from dawn to dusk.

Soon after her arrival, Florence received a letter from Mr. Orr-Ewing authorizing the mission to buy an adjoining plot of land and build a large house on it. One of the church members, Mr. Wang, was put in charge of building a large stone wall around the new property, and Florence was given the money to pay the various workmen that would be required.

Within a week Florence realized that she had a challenge on her hands. Forty workmen showed up to build the seven-foot-high stone wall. Mr. Wang was an elderly Christian, and his chief concern was to preach to the workers. The workers, who were paid by the hour, were more than happy to encourage Mr. Wang to preach to them for hours at a time, and little progress was made on the wall.

Although Florence tried to get Mr. Wang to allow the stonemasons to get on with their work, he found it impossible to stop preaching to them. Eventually Florence sent Mr. Wang on a preaching tour and took over supervising the building process herself.

This led to more frustration as the workmen tried many tricks on Florence, who soon learned that they were chipping the stones into shape by day and stealing them at night. Florence hired a night watchman to watch over the pile of cut stones, but he slept soundly all night and feigned surprise that the pile of stones was growing smaller and smaller each morning. A young schoolboy then offered to watch over the stones at night, and sure enough, he sounded the alarm at 2 A.M. the first night he was on duty.

The three missionary women in the house bounded out of bed and threw on their tunics. Christine was the fastest runner, and she sprinted after the robber, catching him by his queue and dragging him back to the mission house. There she and Florence reprimanded the man and warned him that if they ever caught him stealing from them again, they would take him to the mandarin. The threat seemed to have the desired effect, and the wall was completed without any more theft.

The next challenge was building the new mission house. Mr. Orr-Ewing had promised to send a male missionary to help with all of the negotiations for the house building, but none could be spared. In the end Florence drew up her own plans for the house and submitted them to the CIM board in Shanghai. The plans were revised, and the superintendent then advised Florence to go ahead and supervise the building project herself.

Florence was reluctant to do this. The stone wall had created so many difficulties for her that she dreaded to think what building an entire house would be like. But the house had to be built, so in the end Florence hired Mr. Iao's son T'ai-ho to help her with the building project, and they boldly began.

The first task was to find a builder to build the house. The mission had budgeted $600 for the purpose, but no builder in An-ren would take on the job for less than $1,000. Eventually Florence found a builder in the country who agreed to come to town and erect the house for $615. The plans called for a nine-room house with balconies back and front. The downstairs would be one large room where meetings could be held, and upstairs would be eight rooms. The plans specified the dimensions of the house in feet, but as there was no standard measurement system in China at the time, Florence and the builder had to agree on how long a foot was. Once this was agreed upon, two five-foot-long measuring rods called *changs* were made, one for the builder and one for Florence so that she could check that the builder was building the house to the proper specifications.

Finally construction of the house began, and stonemasons began to erect the sandstone walls of the first story. When the walls were complete, the builder summoned Florence to approve the beams that would support the upper story. With her chang, Florence measured each beam to make sure it met the specifications called for. Those beams she approved she wrote her initials on. Those beams that did not meet the specifications were set aside, and the builder assured her that not one of them would be used in the construction of the house.

Two days later the beams were in place and the builder was ready to begin construction of the second story. For some reason Florence was suspicious. She asked T'ai-ho if he had personally witnessed the beams being put in place. When he told her he had not, Florence ordered him to get a ladder and check to see that each beam that had been used had her initials written on it. Florence soon learned to her dismay that the builder had used every beam she had rejected.

Florence ordered the builder to take down the rejected beams and replace them with ones that met the specifications called for. This time she watched the men closely as they worked. Once the beams were replaced, work began on the second story.

The roof was to be made of clay tiles, and Florence ordered twenty-five thousand tiles for the purpose. Half were to be delivered by the tile maker to An-ren on December 3, the second half on December 22. When no tiles arrived on December 3, Florence began to worry. Finally on December 13 the tile maker arrived in An-ren, but he brought no tiles with him. He apologized for missing the delivery deadline but assured Florence that the tiles were all made, although for some reason he was unable to deliver them. He asked Florence to send a convoy of wheelbarrows to his tile works to take delivery of the tiles and ferry them to An-ren. But before they could do this, he explained that he needed to be paid in full. This was not a customary practice, and Florence refused to pay him until she had taken delivery of all the tiles. The tile maker protested, but Florence held firm. Finally the tile maker relented, and T'ai-ho arranged for a convoy of eight wheelbarrows to go to the tile works and collect the tiles.

Florence was very frustrated when T'ai-ho reported that when he arrived at the tile works, the tile maker sheepishly admitted that he had not yet made the tiles. The man's son had offended his workers several weeks before, and the men had been on strike since then. To make matters worse, it was now too late in the year to make tiles. Winter was descending on the land, and the tile maker could not produce the sun-baked tiles until the spring. This made Florence furious. The growing mission station desperately needed the extra living space, and now the house would have to lie unfinished through the winter.

Several days later, however, T'ai-ho brought some good news. The tile maker's brother also made tiles, and he had a supply on hand that could be purchased for the roof. Florence quickly bought the tiles and had them brought to An-ren, where the builder got to work installing the roof.

Finally, after much frustration, the new house was complete and the missionaries moved into their new quarters. The new house was set back from the busy street, and Florence marveled at how much quieter it was than the old mission house.

Once the move was complete, the old mission house was remodeled into a larger church meeting hall. Soon after the remodeling was finished, seventeen new converts were baptized at An-ren. This made Florence feel that all of her hard work and the inevitable misunderstandings that came with trying to achieve things in a foreign country had been worthwhile.

In early summer 1900 Florence began to hear rumors of serious fighting in the north. Letters from CIM missionaries followed, telling how many secret societies had been formed with the goal of getting rid of all foreigners from Chinese soil. Florence, Christine, and Emma held a meeting and decided the best thing to do in the face of this new situation was to remain calm and continue to work as usual. This became increasingly more difficult to do, especially after the morning of Sunday, July 15, 1900. At ten o'clock in the morning, Florence was conducting a Bible class for beginners in the old mission house when suddenly two strangers burst into the room. A throng of nosy local people followed them.

One of the strangers gestured to Florence, who quickly asked a student to lead the class in a hymn. While the students sang, Florence led the two men from the meeting room and down a narrow hallway away from the prying throng. As she did so, she felt one of the men slip a note up her sleeve.

Florence continued walking. When they reached the kitchen, she offered the men some rice. While they ate, she turned her back to the window, away from the faces that now peered in at them, and read the note. The note, written by Dr. Judd, a fellow missionary upriver, was short and to the point:

> Miss Young, The provincial magistrate here at Rao chco Fu has received an edict from the Empress ordering the extermination of all foreigners and offering a reward of money or official position to anyone who helps to kill us. The magistrate has promised me that he will keep this edict secret for three days in order for us to escape, but after that he must announce it to the people. He has urged me to flee immediately, and to warn you and the others to do the same.

Florence drew a deep breath and reminded herself once again that panicking was the worst thing to do in an emergency. She thanked the messengers for visiting her, slipped the message back up her tunic sleeve, and returned to the Bible study. By now the meeting had ended, and the crowd had moved on into the chapel for the morning church service. Florence breathed a prayer of thanks that Mr. Wang was scheduled to preach at the service. It would give the missionaries time to decide what they should do next.

Half an hour later Florence was back in the kitchen, this time with Christine and Emma. The women fastened the shutters on the window, lit a lamp, and huddled together. Florence handed the note around for each woman to read. "We will need to speak softly," she said when they had read it.

Every aspect of the note was discussed, and the three women came to the conclusion that they should await instructions from the mandarin who was in charge of the nearby town of Kuei-k'i. The mandarin supported the thriving China Inland Mission station in Kuei-k'i, and the women knew that he would alert the missionaries straight away if things were as serious as Dr. Judd supposed them to be. In the meantime they agreed that two new European workers who were passing through An-ren should continue on their way south immediately. There was no reason to put anyone in unnecessary jeopardy. It took several days to arrange for them to leave, and on July 27 Florence wrote to her sister Emily:

> It was a great relief when they were gone. The responsibility of other people's lives is very heavy.... Rumors and threats are flying

about. We go to bed each night with everything prepared for sudden flight. We have a ladder by the wall, and a few clothes entrusted to a friend of Siu-li; but we are so hemmed in that it is impossible to do anything secretly in China.... I cannot write more now; and perhaps it is as well. "It is better *to trust,*" and better *to praise*; and we have been doing both.... Poor China! The people are full of fears and lying reports. If it is so here, so far from the scene of real conflict, how terrible it must be in North China.

As Florence signed the letter and slid it into an envelope, she did not know that the empress's edict was being pasted up on the public walls of An-ren. By morning the town was divided between those who wanted to kill the missionaries and those who were sympathetic toward them. Since the edict extended across all of China, Florence felt that she was probably safer staying in An-ren than traveling through unknown territory to the coast. At the best of times, bands of robbers made the trip dangerous, and now every foreigner's head had a price on it.

Florence soon learned that Dr. and Mrs. Judd had made a similar decision, but things had not gone well for them. Their CIM station was attacked, and they barely escaped with their lives. Their Chinese helpers went into hiding, and one by one they made their way to An-ren, as did the workers from one of Florence's outstations. More bad news soon followed. The Catholic mission at Rao-cheo was burned to the ground, and thirteen missionaries and their children were murdered north of An-ren.

Two nights later a special messenger arrived at midnight with an urgent telegram from CIM headquarters in Shanghai. All women missionaries and children were to make their way to the coast as quickly as possible. Florence understood why. Shanghai was a treaty port protected by well-armed foreign troops. People would be safe there from the turmoil in the rest of the country.

Florence and the other missionaries were unsure which route they should take to Shanghai. Should they brave the Shuihong region, which was always dangerous to foreigners, or go downriver via Takut'ang, where the CIM mission station had just been looted and destroyed? Either route could lead them to safety or to certain death. Which one should they take?

Chapter 10

A New Direction

Within hours the decision of which route to follow was taken out of Florence's hands. The mission sent word that it had secured a boat and sent it downriver from Kuei-k'I, picking up the women missionaries as it passed their stations.

On August 9, as Florence stepped onto the boat, her heart was breaking. She had grown very attached to the people of An-ren in the three years she had lived among them. She had worked hard and seen the number of converts grow steadily, and now she had to leave them. She hoped they would be spared the persecution of Christians that was taking place in other parts of China as antiforeign groups tried to rid China of foreign influence, including "foreign" religion. Florence said a somber good-bye to the Christians of An-ren, and then the boat set off down river.

Since they were passing through hostile territory, the boat stayed in the middle of the Kuang-sin River as it made its way along. That way they hoped to avoid attack from angry bands of Chinese men along the riverbank. Instead of stopping at night and tying up along the riverbank, as was the custom, the boat kept sailing downstream night and day.

Finally, three days after setting out from An-ren, the boat reached Kiu-Kiang, a small treaty port on the river. There a gunboat floated in the river and troops kept the port secure. Florence, Christine, and Emma waited in Kiu-Kiang for one long week until they were able to get passage on a riverboat to Shanghai. They arrived in Shanghai unharmed and made their way to the China Inland Mission headquarters. Hundreds of other missionaries had done the same thing, and although CIM had rented several other houses, there was barely room for three more missionaries. Florence found herself sharing a house with fifty other men, women, and children. Each of the missionaries had bits of information about his or her mission station and the surrounding areas. Slowly they were able to piece together a picture of what had happened in the countryside.

The terrible persecution that foreigners and Chinese Christians had endured was soon dubbed the Boxer Rebellion, after the antiforeign movement known as I Ho Ch'uan, or the righteous, harmonious fists. When the numbers were tallied, the China

Inland Mission had lost fifty-eight missionaries and twenty-one children. Nearly half the Protestant missionaries in the country had been killed. Two thousand Chinese Protestants had also lost their lives in the rebellion. The Chinese Catholics fared even worse, with at least twenty thousand of them losing their lives.

Hudson Taylor was not in China during the Boxer Rebellion, but he sent letters of support and condolence to the missionaries there. Florence wished she could have met with him in person and talked to him about her future. No one at CIM headquarters had any idea when or whether missionaries would be allowed back to their mission stations.

In Shanghai, Florence found a letter from her brother Ernest waiting for her. In the letter Ernest told how their sister Emily was very ill with heart trouble and asked Florence to consider coming home on furlough. Florence took this as a sign that she should leave China, for a few months at least, and return to Australia.

Florence set sail from Shanghai with a group of other missionaries and reached Brisbane on October 25, 1900. When she arrived, she found that her sister was doing a little better and was planning a trip to England with her daughter Olive. Florence was invited to join them on the journey, and she happily agreed to go. They were not due to leave for England for two months, and Florence used the time to check on the progress of the Queensland Kanaka Mission.

Florence was delighted with what she found. The work around Bundaberg had blossomed. Three new mission centers at Hapsberg, Gin Gin, and Avondale had been opened, and there was hardly a Kanaka man in the area who was not learning to read the Bible. And just before Florence arrived back in Australia, three new European workers had set out to establish Bible classes near Cairns. Twelve European missionaries and three Kanakas were now working with the mission.

In addition, John Southey and Walter Fricke had visited North Queensland the year before and taken three of the most faithful Kanaka Christians with them. Each of these men, Charley Aurora, Jack Aoba, and Thomas Sandwich, took a job on a northern plantation so that they could all continue the work of the mission in the evenings and on weekends. As a result, the work of the mission had spread not only to Cairns but also to Port Douglas and Johnstone River. All in all, the three native workers were now conducting Bible and reading classes for 375 indentured laborers, and the number of men attending class was growing each week. Florence was amazed at the growth of the mission during the three years she had been away.

When it came time to depart for England, much to Florence's dismay, Emily was not well enough for a sea voyage. However, Florence's family encouraged her to make the trip anyway, as her niece Olive needed a chaperone and Florence herself needed a long rest to get over the strain of the past three years in China.

With some reluctance, Florence set out with Olive in March 1901. Upon their arrival in England, friends and relatives welcomed them. While Olive rushed around seeing the various sites of England, Florence stayed in the country enjoying the peace and quiet. While in England, Florence attended a large Christian convention called Keswick and was asked to speak to the conference goers for five minutes about her missionary work. She hardly knew where to start, as eighteen years of mission work had to be condensed into five minutes of talking. Still, she did her best, and many of those who heard Florence speak told her how moved they were by the persistence and determination she demonstrated.

While Florence was at the Keswick Convention, one of the women participants invited her and Olive to come to Switzerland for a visit to her chalet in the Chamonix Valley at the foot of Mont Blanc. Florence accepted the invitation right away, as she recognized the name of the region. It was the same region where Hudson Taylor and his wife, Jennie, were spending the winter.

Once in Switzerland, Florence was delighted to see the Taylors again, although she was shocked at how frail Hudson looked. The CIM missionary deaths in China had taken a heavy toll on him.

Olive loved the Alps and tried her hand at every sport she could find. She went luging, ice-skating, and skiing, while Florence preferred quiet walks through the woods with Hudson.

As spring approached, Florence finally felt rested. After talking with Hudson, she was confident of one thing—God wanted her to work in Queensland, at least for the next few years.

Florence said a sad farewell to Hudson Taylor. She was sure she would never see him again. She set out for Marseilles, France, where she and Olive would catch an ocean liner bound for Australia. They arrived in Sydney in mid-April 1902, having been away for just over a year. Upon her arrival back in Australia, Florence was relieved to learn that Emily was no worse than when they had left.

Now that Florence had settled on ministering to the Kanakas, she threw herself into the work. Once again the government had passed an act declaring that all Kanaka laborers must return home at the end of their term of indentured labor and that no new Kanakas were to be hired. Florence had no idea whether this act would be undone, as the previous one had been, and whether all the Kanakas would be gone from Queensland in three years. Despite the uncertainty, she busied herself visiting all the Queensland Kanaka Mission locations to meet the new missionaries serving with the mission. The mission in Port Douglas was the farthest away, located over a thousand miles up the coast. On a cold winter's day in July, Florence set out on her latest adventure.

In the shelter of the Great Barrier Reef, the steamer carrying Florence made its way up the coast to Townsville, where a number of passengers disembarked. The ship then moved on farther north to Halifax, where Florence disembarked to visit several Bible classes the mission had begun in the area. To get to one of the Bible classes, Florence had to ford the Herbert River, where crocodiles were known to lurk in the slow-moving, murky water. Even though she was on horseback, Florence was reluctant to guide her horse into the river and cross it. Her guide spent several minutes reassuring her that despite there being crocodiles in the river, to his knowledge no one fording the river at this point had ever been attacked and killed by the reptiles. Florence did not want to be the first, but eventually, still dubious of the guide's confidence that everything would be all right, she gingerly rode her horse into the river. She soon learned that the guide was right. No menacing crocodile came to make a meal of her, and Florence emerged on the opposite bank of the Herbert River wet but alive.

Five miles beyond the river, Florence's courage was rewarded as she watched eighty-four Kanaka men show up for Bible study and reading class that night.

Following the stop in Halifax, Florence boarded another steamer for the rest of her journey up the coast to Port Douglas, where she spent two weeks visiting the Bible studies the mission was running. She was impressed by what she saw. Almost all the Kanakas in the area were learning to read the Bible, and a number of men had already become Christians. Florence returned to Bundaberg satisfied with all that the mission was doing in north Queensland.

It was clear, too, when she returned that there would be no reprieve for the Kanakas this time. The government was determined to send the men back to their home islands as soon as they had fulfilled the requirements of their labor contracts. The work of the Queensland Kanaka Mission thus took on a new urgency. Florence and the other missionaries working with the mission knew that within three years all of their converts would be back home in the islands. Many of those islands were still steeped in cannibalism and witchcraft.

With indentured servitude on the sugar plantations of Queensland about to wind down, Florence started to ask herself what she should do next. What did God want her to do when all of the Kanakas were finally back on their home islands? One choice was to go back to China, but as she thought about it, another exciting and challenging option began to emerge. Perhaps she could set up a mission in the Pacific islands that would support those Kanaka Christians who had returned home.

This was not an easy option. Missionary work in the islands of Melanesia, where the Kanakas lived, was dangerous. Florence recalled that two years before, in 1900, an independent missionary had gone out to the islands to live and work, but he had died within five months. The climate and the local food proved too much for him. A second man, Robert Ruddell, not knowing that the first missionary was already dead, had gone out to help him. When he learned of the missionary's death, he hitched a ride on a whaleboat and visited a number of islands. Inspired by what he had seen, upon his return to

Queensland, Robert joined the Queensland Kanaka Mission.

Another independent missionary, Joseph Watkinson, had gone out to the islands a year before with a companion, Fred Schwieger. But Fred had died six months later, and Joseph was forced to return to Australia because of a severe case of malaria that he had contracted. Upon his recovery, he too joined the Queensland Kanaka Mission.

Now, as Florence discussed the possibility of opening mission stations in the islands of Melanesia, Robert and Joseph were both enthusiastic about the idea. Their enthusiasm rubbed off on the others serving in the Queensland Kanaka Mission. Soon everyone in the organization was determined to go and help the new Kanaka Christians reach out to their families in the islands.

Finally, at a mission conference in January 1904, it was decided that a Solomon Islands branch of the Queensland Kanaka Mission would be formed. A committee was appointed to oversee the new work, and the committee insisted that Florence become the superintendent of the new branch. By now the deadline for the Kanaka workers to leave Queensland was fast approaching, and Florence felt that this was what God wanted her to do next.

Florence realized that if she was going to lead the work, she needed to see the Solomon Islands for herself. She volunteered to accompany the first group of missionaries going to the Solomon Islands, where they planned to base themselves on the island of Gavutu. The group consisted of three men: Owen Thomas, James Caulfeild, and Hedley Abbott.

Some of the men on the new mission committee questioned the wisdom of a single woman traveling around in the islands. The Solomon Islands could be a treacherous place. But Florence reminded them of some of the situations she had encountered in China. She pointed out that manning her mission outpost during the turbulent days of the Boxer Rebellion proved she was up for the challenge.

The members of the committee finally agreed, though they suggested that Florence take a female companion with her. Helen Fricke, a mother of five children, the youngest just two years old, offered to accompany Florence. At first Florence tried to discourage her. Helen and her family had already sustained the death of her husband, Walter, who had served as superintendent of the mission, and Florence knew that this trip to the Solomon Islands was a dangerous assignment. But Helen was sure that God had called her to go along, so in the end Florence welcomed her company on the trip.

A month of intense preparation for the trip to the Solomon Islands followed. Enough money had been donated to the new branch of the mission to allow for a ten-ton ketch to be built for use in the islands. The new vessel was named the *Daphne,* and a prefabricated mission house was stowed away in her hold to be erected at the new mission station.

The *Daphne* had been built in Sydney, but the vessel was too small to sail all the way from there to the Solomon Islands. So Florence, Helen, and the three men who would staff the new mission station set out for Sydney, where they supervised the *Daphne* being hoisted onto the deck of the SS *Moresby* for the trip to the Solomon Islands. The *Daphne* was lashed down securely to the deck. When the *Moresby* got to Gavutu, a small island off Florida Island in the Solomons, the ketch would be lowered into the water for the missionaries to use.

Four days out from Sydney, Florence was beginning to wonder whether she would ever see land again. The *Moresby* had run into a howling storm in the Tasman Sea, one of the roughest stretches of water in the world. Frothing waves washed across the deck and flowed into Florence's small cabin, which faced out onto the main deck. Soon everything in the cabin was drenched. As the ship pitched and rolled, the captain and the missionaries alike became concerned about the *Daphne*. The ketch strained against the ropes lashing it in place, and on more than one occasion, everyone thought that the vessel was going to break loose and tumble into the angry ocean. To Florence's relief and amazement, it somehow managed to stay put.

As the ship sailed past Lord Howe Island, the storm began to abate. By the time it reached Norfolk Island, the weather was bright and sunny and Florence was able to go ashore for the day while cargo was unloaded from the *Moresby* for the residents of the island.

From Norfolk Island they sailed north into the tropics, and Florence soon discovered how poorly suited to the tropics the *Moresby* was. The vessel was poorly ventilated, and there were few places on board where the passengers could cool off. To make matters worse, forty-five pigs were housed in a pen on the main deck outside the door to Florence's cabin. Not only did the animals squeal constantly, but in the tropical heat, they also began to stink, filling her cabin with an unbearable stench that made it nearly impossible to be inside.

Despite the perils and extreme discomfort of the voyage, Florence contented herself by keeping her eye on the goal of assisting the thousands of returning Kanakas to share the gospel in their homeland. By late March 1904, to her delight, the *Moresby* was finally approaching the Solomon Islands.

Chapter 11

The Solomon Islands

On March 25, 1904, Florence sat on a barrel on the deck of the SS *Moresby* looking out over the Pacific Ocean as the ship navigated its way among the Solomon Islands. With great anticipation she wrote in her journal:

> Our first sight of Malaita!... At 6 A.M. we were passing the SW coast of San Christoval [Cristobal]. At 8 A.M. we sighted Guadalcanar [Guadalcanal], and 10:10 A.M. saw Malaita. Since then we have been steaming all day past San Christoval, Marau Sound, and the NE coast of Guadalcanar, with Malaita clearly visible in the distance.

Three days later the missionaries landed on the small island of Gavutu. The entire island was a trading station owned by a Captain Svenson, who ran a coaling and watering station for the British naval vessels that patrolled the waters of the newly declared British protectorate. Captain Svenson greeted the missionaries and offered to make them as comfortable as possible.

The only house on the island was a long two-storied building with an unlined iron roof. Florence and Helen were given a room on the second floor of the house. When they were shown around the trading post, Florence's heart sank. None of the eighteen huge water tanks had lids. It was no wonder that malaria was so prevalent in these islands.

The *Daphne* had been damaged by the high seas and intense tropical sun on the trip from Sydney and needed repairs to the sail and hull planks before it was fit to sail. Once the prefabricated house was unloaded from the boat's hold onto the island, Owen, James, and Hedley set to work on the ship's repairs. Soon the *Daphne* was ready for her maiden voyage to Malaita, one of the larger islands of the Solomon group. Several local men were hired to sail the ketch, with Owen serving as captain, since he was the only missionary with any sailing experience. Fifteen hours after they set out from Gavutu, Florence spotted a huge white cloud. Owen explained that each of the large Pacific islands had a cloud that hung over the trees and mountains of the landmass. Sure enough, as they sailed closer, the west coast of the island of Malaita emerged from under the cloud. Malaita was a large, mountainous island one hundred miles long, with mountain peaks that reached up four thousand feet from the sea.

As the *Daphne* sailed closer to Malaita, it passed a small inhabited island. The residents of the island beckoned for the missionaries to come ashore. The missionaries dropped anchor, clambered into a rowboat, and went ashore. On the beach the people crowded around them. The dark-skinned natives were naked, and most of the men had shards of bone and shells threaded through their noses and ears and bands of shells and leaves tied around their legs just above their knees. The natives were particularly intrigued by Florence and Helen, never having seen white women before. They crushed in around them and clamored to touch the two women. They explained that they were saltwater people and that the island offered them refuge from the fearsome bushmen that lived on Malaita. The people lived in small huts made from coconut fronds that lined a muddy track leading across the island. As Florence walked around the small village, children and pigs scattered in front of her.

After the visit to the island, the *Daphne* sailed north along the west coast of Malaita toward the village of Malu, where several Christian Kanakas had returned from Queensland. As they made their way along, a large dugout canoe approached the ketch. Florence and Owen were not sure whether the men in the canoe had friendly intentions or not.

"Come on, let's sing," Florence finally urged. "That's one way to find out what their intentions are."

"O for a thousand tongues to sing my great Redeemer's praise," she began belting out.

The others on board soon joined in.

"The glories of my God and King, the triumphs of His grace," they all sang.

A cheer went up from the men in the canoe, and spray flew off their paddles as they raced toward the *Daphne*. They laughed and sang as they came alongside the ketch. As they approached, Florence instantly recognized many of the men. They had been laborers on the sugar plantations in Queensland. How good it was to see their shining faces again.

Shouting above the sound of the ocean as it lapped against the side of the *Daphne*, the men in the canoe explained that they were on their way south to Taravania. They were taking food to a missionary outpost they had just opened there. Before long the men were on their way again, waving and exclaiming how glad they were to be the first islanders to welcome the missionaries and their ship to Malaita.

Two hours after encountering the canoe, the *Daphne* dropped anchor in the lagoon off Malu and went ashore. A crowd of islanders soon gathered around to shake the missionaries' hands. The entire community then escorted the missionaries through the forest to a Christian village at the top of a nearby hill. Florence walked beside Peter Ambuofa, who had been a laborer on the Kalkie plantation at Bundaberg. Peter had been one of the mission's early converts, and Florence had heard snippets of information about him in the ten years since he had left Queensland. But now as they walked together, Peter told Florence his entire story since returning to Malaita.

"When I came back, I think me land'im Urasi, but father'im kill me, 'im see me."

Florence nodded. She knew that Peter was the second son of a bush chief who was very opposed to Christianity. She had no doubt that his father would have killed him had he seen him.

"The chief Urasi, say'im me, 'You sleep under hut with 'im pigs.' I say, 'My Jesus He been come down along place belong stable. Me all right, thank you.' So I pull'im out rubbish, I sleep there. Then the chief he say, 'Run away along or men kill me.' I think hymn, 'Jesus of Nazareth passeth by,' and I cry and I go out and I pass by. I go away, get'im Malu."

"The people of Malu, they are your people, aren't they?" Florence asked.

"Yes'im. No like me here. Four years I praying in hut on sand. Then men come to kill me. I say them, 'Suppose you kill'im me, I go home along heaven.'"

Florence stopped for a minute to catch her breath. The climb up to the village was steep, with many tree roots in the path.

Peter went on to tell Florence that the men of the village had drawn guns on him. Just as they were about to shoot, they heard a peal of thunder and heavy rain began to fall. The rain wet the gunpowder, and the men went away shaking their heads, convinced that some great power protected Peter.

Peter continued to tell Florence about other wonderful things that had happened during that four-year period. He had made a garden, which had flourished even during a drought. The people began to think that he was blessed, especially when their own crops failed. First the children, then the women and men, came to him for food. Peter fed them all and still had some food left over. Florence was also touched to hear that he had written John 3:16 on a piece of paper and fastened it to a tree. He agreed that no one else on the island could speak English. "But I think, might God He see, and might devil he see, and might he say 'Man belong God here, more better I clear out!'"

Florence laughed. It took four years, but the devil finally got the message. Now Peter was the head of a thriving Christian village.

Finally the procession of missionaries and locals reached the village at the top of the hill. Peter led them into a large, open church building, and the entire village of about two hundred people thronged around and began singing hymns to officially welcome the missionaries to their village.

During the next week, Florence and the other missionaries helped Peter where they could. They ran several Bible classes and began reading lessons for the people of the village. They also taught them some new hymns from a hymnal that Owen had brought with him. Florence was impressed by the way Peter and the other Christian leaders in the community were overseeing the village.

By the end of their week in Malu, all of the missionaries had contracted malaria. They were supposed to continue on with their voyage around the island of Malaita to find the most suitable site for another mission station, but the illness prevented them from doing this. And even if they had wanted to continue on, they could not find a crew of island men to sail the *Daphne*. The men who had sailed the vessel from Gavutu had disappeared into the bush.

Finally some saltwater men, as those who lived near the ocean were called, offered to sail the *Daphne* back to Gavutu the next day. That night, however, Florence could not sleep. She felt something was amiss and spent the night praying that God would show her what was wrong. By morning she was convinced that they should not employ the saltwater men to sail the ketch.

That same morning an elderly Christian man named Charley Lofia came to see Florence. Charley explained that he had overheard the would-be sailors talking among themselves. The sailors planned to run the *Daphne* aground on a reef, murder the missionaries, and loot the vessel.

"I no sleep," Charley explained. "God He been talking along my heart. He been say, 'You go along *Daphne* and look out for Miss Young.'"

Florence looked at the faithful old man with gratitude. He had probably saved their lives, and although he was a bushman, he was prepared to take his chances on a white man's ship. Tears slid down her cheeks as she thought of his devotion to them.

Charley convinced two other Christian men to sign up as crew on the *Daphne*. One was a bushman and the other a saltwater man who knew how to sail.

The next day Florence and the other missionaries and the three island crew members said good-bye to Peter Ambuofa and the Christians of Malu and sailed off. The plan, when they reached Gavutu, was for Florence and Helen to connect with the *Ysabel*, a steamer that would transport them back to Australia, while Hedley, Owen, and James would return to Malu to help the Christians there. On the way back to Gavutu, they stopped in at Taravania to deliver gifts to the people there from the church at Malu. Then they set out in a westerly direction for Gavutu.

The journey to Gavutu was grueling and treacherous. The *Daphne* was constantly becalmed, and on several occasions the ocean current pushed the ketch dangerously close to the jagged coral reefs. To make matters worse, the Solomon Islands were situated eight degrees from the equator, and the hot tropical sun baked down mercilessly on those in the boat, burning their skin and further weakening their malaria-wracked bodies.

Soon Helen was lying on the deck on one side of the boat while Hedley lay on the other side, both with dangerously high temperatures. Florence herself felt weak and wanted to lie down on the deck with the others, but she pushed herself on, cooking rice and boiling drinking water for the crew. Finally, on the fifth day, Gavutu appeared on the horizon, but by then Owen had lapsed into unconsciousness at the wheel. James, who had no sailing experience, and the makeshift crew of three island men were forced to guide the *Daphne* in failing light amid the reefs that guarded the entrance to the harbor on Gavutu. Eventually, after grazing a reef with the keel of the boat they managed to moor it alongside the dock.

Florence could hardly believe that they had arrived at all, between the becalmings, the heat, and malaria. It was ten o'clock in the evening by then, and everyone aboard the *Daphne* was too exhausted to transfer to land, so they all collapsed onto the deck of the boat, where they slept one more night.

In the morning the missionaries made a supreme effort to get themselves ashore. James went first, taking Helen by the arm and guiding her off the boat, while the men from Malu helped Owen and Hedley ashore. Florence stayed behind for a few more minutes to gather the clothes and utensils they would need over the next several days. When she climbed up on deck, she saw that James and Helen had gone only a few feet along the dock before they had both fainted. She left the pile of clothes and utensils on deck and went to their aid. She managed to rouse James, and together he and Florence managed to get Helen to Captain Svenson's house and into bed.

For the next seven weeks the missionaries took turns nursing each other as their malarial fevers came and went. At the end of seven weeks, the HMS *Pylades* stopped at Gavutu to take on coal. The vessel had a British doctor aboard who advised Florence that Owen was so sick that he should be taken back to Australia as quickly as possible. However, this was not easily done. The *Ysabel*, the ship they had been waiting for to take them to Australia, had failed to arrive at Gavutu, leaving Florence stranded. Finally a whaleboat appeared in the harbor, bringing the news that the *Ysabel* had lost its propeller near the northern end of Malaita and lay at anchor waiting for help to arrive. There was nothing to do but wait for some other ship headed south to arrive at Gavutu. Eventually the SS *Morseby* stopped at the island to take on more coal for its trip to Sydney, and the captain agreed to take Florence, Helen, and Owen on board. The three of them stood on deck, bracing themselves against the railing as they watched the *Daphne* fade from view.

Once at sea Owen began to feel a little better, though Helen and Florence were both very ill. By the time they arrived back in Sydney sixteen days later, Florence was glad to put herself into the hands of her doctor nephew, Northcote Deck. She had lost thirty pounds in the weeks she'd been away, and her temperature was spiking to 106 degrees.

As she lay between the smooth white cotton sheets at her nephew's house, Florence wondered how the men on board the *Daphne* back in the Solomon Islands were faring. She had no idea that it would be six months before the two men would be well enough and able to engage a new crew to make it back to Malu.

Chapter 12

The Eastern Side of the Island

Six weeks after leaving Gavutu, Florence stood in the doorway of a neatly though sparsely furnished seven-room cottage.

"It's perfect!" she declared, turning to Ernest. "Really, I can't thank you and Arthur enough."

Florence meant the words with all her heart. While she had been away in the islands, her brothers had built the cottage for her at Fairymead. The cottage was located in the Bush Paddock, halfway between the plantation house and the huts of the Kanaka workers.

"Living here will cut down so much on Kathleen's and my workloads," she continued, walking through the kitchen and noting the indoor water pump in the sink. "A house this size won't take much running at all, and we have only a few hundred yards to walk to class. When it's cool enough, we'll even be able to have classes on the veranda."

"I thought you'd like it," Ernest beamed. "And you can thank Kathleen for the water pump. She was the one who insisted on all the latest gadgets."

Florence turned and put her arm around her niece. "Thanks for that, and so much more. The work here is going so well with you at the helm. There is no way I would have felt comfortable leaving without knowing you were here."

Kathleen turned red. "We are all doing what we can," she replied modestly.

As the weeks passed, it seemed as if there was more to do than ever before. While the government was still sticking to its plan to send all the Kanakas back home to the islands, under pressure from the sugarcane growers it had pushed back the deadline to December 31, 1906. And now that she had seen firsthand the situations that the men were going home to, Florence worked harder than ever. She lay in bed at night thinking of new ways to teach the men to read. She knew that reading would help them understand the gospel better so that their faith would remain strong, no matter what happened to them when they returned home.

Every so often a letter arrived from James or Hedley in the Solomons. Florence prayed earnestly for them as she read of the struggles that they were enduring trying to sail back to Malu in the *Daphne*. They had had difficulty getting together a crew. James wrote that whenever a crew was available, Grant, the seaman they had put in charge of sailing the vessel, declared that the weather was unfavorable. Then the crew would disappear and were nowhere to be found when the weather was declared perfect for sailing.

To compound their frustrations, Hedley had come down with a severe fever and returned to Sydney for medical treatment. The voyage home, however, had improved his health, and he had gone back to Gavutu on the return voyage.

It was not until Christmastime that James and Hedley were finally able to sail the *Daphne* back to Malu. Letters from the two missionaries then became more positive. Peter Ambuofa helped them find a suitable site for a mission station, and a native hut was erected on the spot and a school started immediately.

Meanwhile, Florence was preparing to make her second visit to the Solomon Islands. She left Australia in early July 1905, along with Jane Foster, a long-time missionary friend from her days in the China Inland Mission. Florence met James and Hedley and a new missionary, Joseph Watkinson, at Aola, on the island of Guadalcanal. She was delighted to find the *Daphne* in fine condition. Some improvements had even been made to the vessel, which now had a stove in the galley and a ventilator in the cabin. The rice and water no longer needed to be boiled over a fire in a tin on the deck.

The plan during Florence's visit was to sail the *Daphne* around to the eastern side of Malaita to scout out a site for another mission station. However, the

British official in charge at Aola warned them not to go that way. "The people are worse than ever," he said. "There are killings all the time. It would be thoroughly unsafe for you to go there."

Florence found herself in a quandary. She did not want to risk her life and the lives of the others unnecessarily, but she felt strongly that they should expand their mission stations into the most needy areas. And what, she asked herself, could be more needy than people living in utter spiritual darkness? It was at times like this that Florence was grateful that she had been a part of the China Inland Mission. Hudson Taylor's wise words often came back to her. On this occasion she recalled a time in Shanghai when someone had asked Taylor about the wisdom of sending single women to live alone in inland China.

"Yes," Taylor had replied, "there may be danger, but you see, they have the Lord of Hosts with them, and that makes all the difference."

With those words in her heart, Florence decided to visit the eastern side of the island and trust that God would keep them safe. On July 20, 1905, Florence wrote in her diary:

> We left…at 3 A.M., and in a few minutes were tossing on a very rough sea. The cabin was an abode of misery. Two seasick passengers clinging frantically to their berths, and a perfect bombardment of tins, pannikins, bottles etc., flying about! Provisions, trade-goods, and

crockery are all stored in the cabin....Swarms of cockroaches abound. Every now and then Mr. Abbott's cheery whistle or a few words of encouragement came to our help; but we were thankful to reach Bia-kwa in the Lagoon. It was some consolation that the trip was reckoned a very rough one. One sea [wave] splashed to the top of the mainsail and the jib was carried away.

The *Daphne* lay at anchor off Bia-kwa while the ripped sails were repaired, and four days later they sailed into One Pusu, halfway along the west coast of Malaita. Florence continued recording in her journal what she saw.

> The entrance [to the harbor] is very narrow; so we anchored outside till the wind lessened, and then rowed into a beautiful harbour, perfectly sheltered from all winds. The Christian village on the northern end of the peninsula contains only three houses with a canoe house and a tiny church, all built under young coconut trees. Barnabas [one of the Kanaka men from Fairymead] was soon on board. He and George [another Kanaka from Queensland] have been working here for four or five years, and have won the friendship of some of the bush people, who have built a village on the mainland just opposite to protect them. It seems a suitable

place for the head station; only 35 miles from Aola (where the steamer calls) and well exposed to both NW and SE winds.... About four acres have been cleared for two years, which will save time and health, as the sun and air have sweetened the ground. The land is low, and the soil broken coral, suitable only for coconuts. But sweet potatoes can also be grown.

Florence and the other missionaries were thrilled to find another Christian village established as a direct result of their work among the Kanakas back in Queensland. They held a special church service with Barnabas and George to honor them for their hard work and constant faith. They also visited the bush people, who, even though they were not Christians, were glad to welcome the missionaries to the area and invite them to stay.

At the end of three days, Florence was certain that One Pusu would indeed be a good location for their main mission station in the Solomon Islands, and she promised Barnabas that they would be back soon to work out some of the details for establishing the station.

After the visit to One Pusu, they set sail down the coast, hoping to navigate their way through the narrow Maramasike Passage that would take them to the east coast of the island. Things did not go as planned. They made it to Uhu, twenty-two miles down the coast from One Pusu, by 11:00 A.M. on

July 27 and decided to press on the extra nine miles to the opening of the Maramasike Passage. However, the southeasterly trade winds suddenly died down at 1:00 P.M., and the *Daphne* was becalmed.

The boat bobbed on the ocean swell like a cork, and the current began to carry it toward the jagged coral reef. The missionaries huddled on the deck and began to pray for God's protection. As they prayed, they felt a gentle puff of wind, but it was not enough to fill the *Daphne*'s sails and move her along. As they continued to pray, more puffs of wind arose until a steady gentle breeze was blowing. This was enough to fill out the ketch's sails, and slowly they began to move away from the menacing reef. By 4:00 P.M. they lay at anchor in the sheltered entrance to Maramasike Passage.

The following morning they set off through the passage. The first half of the Maramasike Passage was narrow, with steep, jungle-covered cliffs rising from the water's edge. Once through this narrow stretch, the passage widened, but as it did, the water got shallower and there were many sandbars to navigate around. At one point they ran aground on one of the sandbars, but a large gust of wind managed to pull them free. Florence was glad about this, because within the jungle on either side of the passage, she had noticed natives skulking with guns and spears in hand.

Finally they were through the passage, and by Saturday afternoon the *Daphne* lay at anchor at Takataka. At last they were on the eastern side of the island. Florence and the others aboard saw many dark figures in the shadows of the bush along the beach, and several canoes set out to visit the boat. These, it turned out, were filled with Kanaka men who had heard that Florence might be coming to the area on a boat and were eager to meet her and inquire about friends who had gone home to other islands. That evening Florence heard calls and signals from the shore. She knew that war parties could be gathering to paddle out and attack them, but there was nothing she could do about it but pray. The missionaries had deliberately decided against having a single gun aboard the ketch and so were defenseless should they be attacked. Despite the danger, Florence slept well, with the water of the lagoon gently slapping against the hull of the *Daphne*.

The next morning they sailed on up the east coast to Manakwoi, where a local chief came to greet them. He, too, had been at Fairymead, although he had never accepted the gospel message himself. Still, his first words were, "We want'im school very much. Suppose man come, teach us, we look after him, give him tucker [food], make house for him. Me want'im school very much!"

Florence promised to do what she could, and the *Daphne* sailed on. It was after midnight before they reached Sinorango and dropped anchor in the sheltered harbor for the night. Early the next morning a single canoe paddled up to the ketch. In the canoe was one of the Kanaka teachers from the Geraldton plantation in Queensland. He had feathers tucked in his hair, and he wore many rings on his fingers and shells in his ears and nose.

"Sam!" Florence exclaimed. "We were hoping to find you."

She tried to keep smiling, although she was very distressed by what she saw. Sam's only clothing was a calico loin cloth, on which were printed several verses of the book of Jonah. Florence instantly recognized the fabric; it was the calico on which Owen Thomas had printed wall charts of Bible stories. Owen had given these to his Kanaka teachers when they returned to their islands.

Sam Faralati had a sad story to tell as to why he was wearing the wall chart instead of using it to teach reading. He told Florence that it had been very difficult for him since returning to preach to his people. A band of troublemakers had destroyed his boat and stripped him of all of his clothing. He had no choice but to use the calico wall chart to fashion something to cover himself with. "I can't lose'im Jesus, but I no been keep Him close up," he admitted sadly.

Florence encouraged Sam to come back to Malu with them so the Christians there could rekindle his missionary zeal. Sam gladly agreed to go along, and the *Daphne* set sail northward along the coast with him on board. They made several more stops, searching for suitable sites for future mission stations, before they reached Malu.

It was a great day when they finally reached Malu. Florence was delighted to have proved the

British official wrong. It was possible to sail around the eastern side of Malaita and live to tell about the experience.

Florence was also delighted to see that everything was going well at Malu. Heavy work had been done clearing the site on a spot three hundred feet above the sea where the new mission station was to be built. Also, a road had been hacked out of a steep hillside to get up to the site. The native workers had not neglected their missionary calling in order to get the work done. They had been waiting for Florence and the others to arrive so that they could have one big baptismal service.

On Sunday, August 13, 1905, twenty-five local men and women were baptized in the river. Over two hundred people from the Malu area gathered to witness the event. This brought the total number of baptized Christians in the village to seventy-five. Some of them had been converted in Queensland, but most of them had heard the gospel for the first time on their own island.

Twelve days later the *Daphne* sailed out of Malu with Florence, Jane, Hedley, Joseph, and eleven native Christians aboard. The plan was for the *Daphne* to cross the Indispensable Straits and drop Florence and Jane off at Gavutu before sailing on to One Pusu to set up the new station.

Manu, one of the native Christians aboard, was escaping a death threat. His father had been a village chief when a power struggle developed in the tribe. The chief had been killed, along with all of his children except for Manu and one of his sisters. The Christians at Malu had rescued them both and offered to get them to One Pusu, where they would be out of reach of their enemies.

Before reaching Gavutu, the *Daphne* encountered a fierce storm and was tossed from side to side in the heaving sea as waves crashed across her deck. Florence, fearing she might be washed overboard, lashed herself to the forward hatch cover with a rope for the duration of the storm.

Thankfully, the storm finally abated, and they arrived in Gavutu. There, Florence was able to arrange for Captain Svensen to deliver to One Pusu the prefabricated house they had brought with them from Sydney in the hold of the *Daphne* on the previous trip.

With perfect timing, a steamer bound for Australia arrived at Gavutu for recoaling the following day, and Florence and Jane bought passage home on the vessel.

Florence returned to Fairymead with fresh enthusiasm for equipping the remaining Kanakas so they could be strong missionaries when they returned to their own islands. Now only fifteen months were remaining before all the Kanakas were scheduled to leave Australia.

Chapter 13

The Cycle of Violence

Florence left Gavutu for Australia in September 1905, but nine months later she was back on board the *Daphne* in the Solomon Islands. This time she was accompanying Robert and Susan Ruddell and five native teachers to One Pusu.

This voyage from Gavutu to One Pusu and the island of Malaita was even more treacherous than Florence's previous journey across the stretch of water. Once again the *Daphne* was pounded by a storm that sent the boat reeling from side to side while huge waves rolled across her deck. And once again Florence lashed herself to the forward hatch cover with a rope. This time she wrapped herself in a tarpaulin, but it didn't seem to help much, and soon she was drenched.

Even Florence, who was a good sailor, began to wonder whether the *Daphne* might capsize and sink. She was very relieved when, three days after setting out, they finally dropped anchor off One Pusu. It had been a long and harrowing voyage, and Florence wondered whether Susan could ever again be persuaded to climb aboard the *Daphne*.

The workers at One Pusu were experiencing great difficulties as the result of a spate of murders in the area. Once a murder was committed, it was nearly impossible to stop another murder, and then another, in a cycle of retaliation. James Caulfeild explained that the non-Christian islanders believed that every death, even one as a result of sickness or old age, was someone's fault. So when a death occurred, the dead person's relatives consulted a local witch doctor to find out who had "caused" the death. This gave the witch doctor tremendous power in the tribe, because whoever he identified as causing the death would be murdered by the grieving family. Then members of that person's family would come to the witch doctor to find out who it was they should kill for the murder of their loved one, and on and on the cycle went.

To make matters worse, if the person the witch doctor said caused the death could not be found, another member of that person's family could be killed in his or her place. This often resulted in old women and small children being killed.

Just before Florence arrived, one of the workers at One Pusu had been killed for such a reason.

Florence was relieved when Barnabas did not talk about killing someone else in retaliation but instead urged all the Christians to forgive and pray for an end to the cycle of violence.

Despite such brutality going on around them, the Ruddells were eager to become part of the community at One Pusu. Their assignment was to supervise the clearing of fifty acres of land that the mission had leased. The cleared land was to be planted in coconuts, which would be eaten or sold to help support students at the One Pusu Training School for Teachers, which Robert Ruddell was going to establish.

Once the Ruddells were settled in at One Pusu, Florence returned to Queensland. She arrived just in time for the fall gathering of Kanaka Christians at Mackay, on the Queensland coast.

With a mixture of pride and sorrow, Florence watched the last remaining Kanaka Christians in the area worship together. During the gathering a large baptismal service was held, the ninety-second such service the mission had held in Queensland. The baptismal service was followed by a hymn-singing celebration.

The hymn-singing celebration was held in a schoolhouse that could barely contain the 250 people who squeezed into it. A large map of the western Pacific islands had been nailed to the front wall of the schoolhouse, and on it were sixteen small red flags. Three of the flags represented the main mission stations in the Solomon Islands, and the other thirteen flags represented the outstations that had been established. At the meeting Florence was asked to report on what she had seen while in the islands, and everyone listened attentively as she spoke. Florence knew that the men were thinking about what would happen to them when they returned to their home islands.

When Florence finished speaking a ripple went through the audience, and then Mr. Lancaster stood up and waved his hand for Florence to stay where she was at the front.

"Just one moment, Miss Young," he began. "We have all been honored to be a part of the Queensland Kanaka Mission and to serve under your leadership. We know that we are entering the twenty-fifth year since you founded the mission, and we are delighted to present you with this check for 416 pounds, which we collected from five hundred donors. It is to go toward the purchase of a boat with an oil engine to work in Malaita."

Florence gasped. She had no idea that such a collection had been going on while she was away in the islands. With tears in her eyes, she addressed the crowd once again.

"Thank you, thank you," she said. "When I think of the tiny and insignificant beginning of this mission, my heart is filled with gratefulness toward God. I can almost see the tumbledown little building with its shingle roof at Fairymead. There ten men and one woman formed my first class twenty-four and a half years ago. I knew nothing then of missionary work, but the Master had said, 'Preach the gospel to every creature,' and these people had never heard the Good News."

Florence paused for a moment and looked around at all the bright, smiling faces.

"I thank God that beginning was made, and through His grace the work has gone on to this day. How many objections were raised at the beginning! How difficult it seemed. And when no one else would take up the work, my sister-in-law Ellen Young and I went forward together, believing that the little we could do, combined with God's blessing, would be enough.

"Just think, it is only two and a half years since that first visit of the *Daphne,* and now we have a staff of nineteen European missionaries, over one hundred native teachers, a weekly average attendance from six thousand to seven thousand at Bible classes, and best of all, 2,484 men and women have been converted and baptized in the name of the Lord Jesus.

"The work which we began here among the Kanakas is being redirected now toward the islands they are returning to. On my last visit poor Mrs. Ruddell was tried sorely when she was tossed about in high seas. When she got to One Pusu, she told me she was going to pray hard for a vessel with an oil engine, which would make the voyage both safer and more comfortable.

"Thank you all for this wonderful gift. It is an answer to Susan Ruddell's prayers and my prayers, and I know that many of you will be blessed by the vessel when it visits your villages in the future."

Florence found it impossible to sleep that night. She lay in bed and thought about how scared she had been all those years ago to pray out loud and how daunting it had seemed to teach a Bible class to a handful of people. She thought about her mother and father and her sister Constance, and how amazed they would all be at what she had become a part of. She also thought about the last of the Kanaka men going home. It was only a matter of six months now before they would all be gone from Australia. There would be no more gatherings like the one tonight in Queensland.

As the months rolled by toward Christmas, hundreds of Kanaka men left the plantations and made their way to Brisbane to embark on the steamship voyage home. Florence arranged for the Brisbane City Mission to care for the workers and hold meetings while they waited for the steamers to arrive.

It was too heartbreaking for Florence to see the men leave. Instead she went to Sydney to supervise the building of the new boat. She had settled on a ketch-rigged, fifty-five-foot-long yacht with a twenty-horsepower oil engine. Although the boat, which was to be called the *Evangel*, would use wind power as much as possible, the engine would allow the vessel to move against the wind, or in the absence of wind, and make maneuvering to dock much easier.

By the beginning of 1907, there was no more evangelism and teaching work to be done among the

Kanakas in Queensland. As a result, it was decided to change the mission's name from the Queensland Kanaka Mission to the South Sea Evangelical Mission. With the departure of the Kanakas from Australia, all of the European workers with the mission were faced with the same decision: did they now go to the islands to minister to the Kanakas, or did they retire from the mission?

One of the longest serving and most tireless workers with the organization was Florence's niece Kathleen Deck. While she had suffered through poor health for the past twelve years, Kathleen still wanted to go and work in the islands. Unlike most mission directors, who would not send a person in ill health overseas, Florence welcomed Kathleen into this new phase of the work and advised her to do what she could and rest as often as she needed to.

In mid-June 1907 the two women set out on a steamer for Gavutu, where they planned to rendezvous with the *Evangel* as she made her maiden voyage. The *Evangel* had been shipped to the Solomon Islands upon her completion several weeks before. All went according to plan, and Florence and Kathleen transferred to the new mission vessel and set off on a voyage around Malaita. They planned to visit all of the mission's outstations to see what the various needs of the missionaries and teachers serving there were.

Along the way they stopped in at the only mission station on the island of Nggela, located at a place called Tulagi. Florence learned very quickly that sending the Kanakas home had upset the balance of power on the island.

Barnabas had moved from One Pusu to Tulagi to man the station, but things had been very difficult since his arrival. He told Florence of how a local chief had died and in usual fashion a witch doctor was consulted as to the cause of the chief's death. The witch doctor declared that a Kanaka couple named Piri and Polly and Piri's father had conspired together to kill the chief. Piri and Polly were not Christians, but they knew they were in deep trouble, and they fled with Piri's father to the little Christian community on the southern end of the lagoon.

Barnabas explained how he welcomed them and promised to do his best to protect them, though there were no weapons in the community. Soon twenty warriors paddled a large canoe down the lagoon. They stopped on the beach in the distance and lit a huge fire, which would be used to cook the three runaways.

According to Barnabas, he could see the smoke rising from the fire and watched as the warriors got back in their canoe and began paddling closer. There was nothing the Christians could do except pray.

As it turned out, their prayers were answered. At the moment they prayed, a ship sailed into the lagoon and dropped anchor. Barnabas urged the three refugees to board the ship and ask for work, which they did. An hour later the ship sailed away with the three aboard. The warriors, who had watched the events transpire from a distance, were furious and threatened to destroy the whole village.

Then Barnabas lowered his eyes as he spoke. "During the night the village chief, who is not a Christian, became very afraid that the whole village would indeed be destroyed, so he threw his teenage daughter out to the warriors, and she was cooked and eaten the following day."

It was a sobering story, and Florence's heart was heavy. She had the feeling that she would hear many other similar stories before the voyage around Malaita was over. Her feeling proved to be well-founded. The *Evangel*'s next major port of call was Malu. Florence arrived to find the Christian community in mourning. Just four days before, Charley Lofia had been murdered. Charley was a beloved Christian leader who had been the first person to come to Peter Ambuofa's aid on the island. James Caulfeild explained that Peter's parents, who were very antagonistic to the gospel, had consulted a witch doctor, who told them that Charley had caused the death of one of their other sons a year before. When Charley learned of this, he sought refuge with the Christians at Ainiuke. But he had just recently returned to Malu, and as soon as Peter's parents heard that Charley was back, they sent someone down from the bush to murder him.

Florence and Kathleen stayed on at Malu to help comfort the community after Charley's death. They took up residence in the newly completed mission house, a two-room affair built of bamboo and lined with scrim, with a commanding view of Malu, the lagoon, and the ocean beyond.

Despite all the difficulties, the number of Christians at Malu began to grow. Twice each day the local Christians would meet together to pray.

During Florence's stay at Malu, six of the local men came to her and asked if they could be sent out as missionaries to the island of San Cristobal. Florence reminded them that there would be many trials and difficulties ahead for them if they went. Regardless of the dangers ahead, the men all pledged themselves to go and start a mission outpost on San Cristobal or die trying.

Florence and Kathleen, along with the six new native missionaries, set out on the *Evangel* for San Cristobal.

Chapter 14

A Growing Mission

On the evening of May 12, 1909, Florence Young once again stood on the deck of the *Evangel* surveying the coastline, which was illuminated by the full moon. They were entering One Pusu harbor, and Florence's nephew Northcote stood beside her. He had just given up his medical practice in Sydney and joined the mission as a traveling doctor and the trainee captain of the *Evangel*. Florence thought it was a perfect combination, and she was very grateful that her nephew had so many practical skills to offer the mission. She was sure he would quickly become an indispensable part of the work.

Two new missionaries, a woman and a man, were on board with them, as well as two missionaries returning from furlough.

"What are you thinking, Auntie?" Northcote asked Florence.

Florence sighed. "The southeast monsoon is late this year, and I was wondering whether we had time to visit David and Rhoda at Talise."

"That's on the south side of Guadalcanal, isn't it?" Northcote asked.

"Yes," Florence replied, "and seven months of the year it's quite impossible to land on the south side. The sea is rough, and there are no harbors to be found. I know the monsoon could strike any day, but I am worried about David and Rhoda. No one has heard from them in over a year, and the last time James visited them, he said they were disheartened. I really do wish we could go and encourage them."

"Well, should we risk it?" Northcote asked.

"I really think we should," Florence replied. "If we started right away, we might make it in and out before the swells start."

The rush began. First they had to unload the four missionaries and all of their supplies at One Pusu, then check out the *Evangel* for signs of wear and tear from the last voyage, and repack for Talise. By going without sleep, Florence and Northcote achieved their goal in less than twenty-four hours. Northcote's sister Kathleen and Hedley also came along on the trip.

They traveled all of the following night and reached Marau Sound on the eastern tip of Guadalcanal by daybreak and Talise Point by four o'clock the next day. As they approached the point, Florence scanned the shoreline through her binoculars and smiled at the commotion the arrival of the *Evangel* was causing. People were running in all directions. Soon she spotted two adults and two children wading out into the water. As the boat got closer, Florence saw that it was Rhoda and David and their two children, Jessie and Ruth, who were wading out into the water to greet them.

The *Evangel* dropped anchor, and by the time the dinghy made it to shore, a large crowd had gathered to welcome the missionaries. Many pairs of hands grabbed the dinghy and dragged it ashore.

David and Rhoda surrounded Florence and clung to her like a mother. They wept for joy as they introduced her to many of the people crowded around them.

"See," David said to the crowd, "we told you Miss Florence would come and teach us."

Florence could hardly hold back the tears herself. David and Rhoda looked gaunt and weak, yet their dark faces were radiant, especially when they showed her around the new church building. How glad she was that they had taken the risk and visited.

Florence was even happier for the visit after the couple told her of the trials they had been through. They explained how they had been very sick since coming to Talise. Still, they had used what little energy they had to build a large church. David had few tools, so he had split large trees with stones, and when he and Rhoda were too weak to stand, the couple had crawled into the bush and gathered sticks for the walls of the building. The result was a large, airy structure in which twenty natives now attended school regularly. Florence felt humbled by the sacrifices this Kanaka couple had made and the way in which they had endured so many hardships.

That night Northcote brought a "magic lantern" slide projector ashore. Most of the local people had never seen any kind of picture before, much less a slide show. The slide presentation on the story of Jesus drew a huge crowd. As the show proceeded, the chief crept nearer and nearer to the screen until he could touch it. He reached out and tried to grab one of the men on the screen and then danced with delight when he realized it was just a life-sized photograph. As a result of the slide show, several more local people showed an interest in going to school and learning to read about the pictures they had just seen on the makeshift screen.

The following day Florence decided to visit Malahiti, fifteen miles farther west, where David had told her that about a dozen Christians lived. No school was located there, and David was eager to see whether something could be set up for the locals.

David, Florence, and the others set out for Malahiti in the *Evangel,* leaving Hedley behind to teach school for a couple of days. They made it safely to their destination and dropped anchor off Malahiti. Getting ashore proved to be a harrowing experience, however. The coast on this part of the island was windswept and exposed, and the waves crashed against the shore. As the missionaries rowed ashore, they began to wonder whether they would actually be able to land. Large breakers rolled past the rowboat, and Florence feared they might be swamped by them.

A number of natives had gathered on the shore to watch, and they began to yell instructions to the missionaries over the sound of the waves. They knew the currents along the coast well, and they yelled for the men to stop rowing. When several large waves had gone by and crashed ashore, those onshore yelled for the men to row hard, which they did, and the boat cut its way through the water toward the beach. As the boat got close, a number of the local men ran out and grabbed it by the gunwales and pulled it ashore. As the bottom of the boat touched the beach, several more large waves came rolling in, and Florence and the other missionaries had to leap out of the boat and quickly scramble ashore, wet but safe.

The native men gathered around the group and shook their hands, but the native women had never seen a white woman before. When they saw Florence and Kathleen, they screamed in fear and ran into the jungle for cover. Eventually David was able to coax them back to the beach, and slowly their fear subsided. Soon they too were crowded around Florence and Kathleen, touching their white skin and laughing among themselves.

David gathered the local Christians together. Several of the men had worked on the sugarcane plantations in Queensland, and three others had worked on the plantations in Fiji. They held a small service together and prayed and sang several hymns, and then the locals explained how they wanted a missionary to come to their area and start a school. Florence promised to do what she could.

As the sun began to sink over the ocean, it was time for the missionaries to head back to the *Evangel*. Getting off the beach and back to the boat proved as exciting as landing had been. When the sea seemed to quiet for a moment, the locals quickly dragged the boat off the beach and out into the water. When they were chest deep, they told the men to row, which the men did as hard as they could. As the men rowed hard, several waves broke over the bow, drenching everyone in the rowboat. But the men kept rowing, and soon they were beyond the breakers and headed toward the *Evangel*.

Once the missionaries had climbed aboard the boat and changed into some dry clothes, they set out once again to return to Talise. But their dry clothes were soon drenched as the *Evangel* ran headlong into an angry storm. The wind whipped the sea into a frenzy, and torrential rains poured down on them. The *Evangel* pitched and rolled in the swell, and soon everyone aboard was violently seasick. It was a long and harrowing night as everyone huddled together below deck, vomiting and trying to stop too much water from flooding into the cabin.

Finally, in the early hours of the morning, they arrived off Talise. It was too rough to drop anchor, so while the *Evangel* circled off Talise Point, David said good-bye to Florence, thanking her warmly for her visit, and rowed ashore. Two hours later Hedley arrived back at the boat, wet and buffeted by the weather, but safe. They then once again set off into the storm along the coast of Guadalcanal.

As the sun came up over the horizon, Florence was dismayed to see that they were still within sight of Talise Point. They had been battered by the ocean all night long but had made little headway against the storm. All they could do was pray and keep heading west along the coast. Slowly, as the day wore on, the *Evangel* distanced itself from Talise Point, and by nightfall all aboard were grateful to finally reach the safety and shelter of Marau Sound and drop anchor.

The exhausted crew spent the next day, Sunday, at anchor in the sound. Much to Florence's surprise, as the storm finally abated, they spotted a tiny inhabited island not far from where they were anchored. Florence and Northcote decided to investigate the island, where they found a Christian Kanaka who was dying of tuberculosis.

The man's face lit up when he saw Florence, though he had a sad confession to make. "When I come home," he began, "I try tell'im my people about Jesus. They not want Him. By and by I think I lose'im read, and by and by I lose'im pray, and might lose Jesus! But very slowly, I think, might Jesus, Him not been lose'im me."

Florence wiped the man's face with a wet cloth. "That's right," she told him. "The Good Shepherd never loses His sheep. He promises that He will give us eternal life and that no one can ever snatch you out of His hand."

The man raised his feeble head. "You pray'im me?" he asked.

Florence was delighted to pray for the man and marveled that they had found him at all in such a lonely spot.

The *Evangel* finally sailed out of Marau Sound on Tuesday morning and headed on to Wanoni Bay, where they had another successful magic lantern presentation with the local people. Then they set out for Malu.

Joyous news was awaiting them upon their arrival in Malu. It concerned Peter Ambuofa's father, Gosila, and his mother, Ratalo. This couple had arranged the murder of Charley Lofia, but in the time Florence had been away, Gosila and Ratalo had undergone a very drastic change.

Peter explained that some of his relatives had had their lives threatened and took refuge with Gosila and Ratalo in the mountains. After a few days, Ratalo arranged to turn the relatives over to their enemy, and when Gosila learned of her plot, he was very angry. He said he would leave her and go to live with Peter. What's more, he declared that he would go to the school at Malu and learn about the Christian God.

Peter related how shocked he was to see his father and several members of his extended family emerge from the bush and ask to be enrolled in the school. Peter agreed, of course, and Gosila started to read and study the Bible. Other chiefs in the area taunted him. "It is a terrible thing to see a man like you giving up all of your power and living like a poor man," they told him. But Gosila did not care and would not be dissuaded from learning.

Within a short time, Gosila began to change and confessed that he wanted to spend the rest of his life serving God. Peter and the other Christians at Malu forgave him for arranging for Charley's murder and took him into their hearts as a Christian brother. Seeing the tremendous change in Gosila, Ratalo soon arrived in Malu wanting to learn to read the Bible. She, too, soon became a Christian. As Florence returned to Sydney to take care of mission business, the story left her feeling grateful for the faithful Kanaka Christians.

So much had to be done now that the number of missionaries serving with the mission was rapidly growing. Every single thing they needed, from medicines to books, flour, and rope, had to be purchased in Sydney, crated up, and sent out to the islands. It was a huge task, and along with bookkeeping and letter writing, it kept Florence very busy.

Florence prayed daily for the workers in the islands and eagerly awaited mail from them. Sometimes a letter brought encouraging news, like the letter that arrived telling of an elderly Kanaka man whom no one had heard from in the eighteen years since he had left Fairymead, in Queensland. His name was Samuel Jacko, and although he could read only a little and could not write at all, he had gathered his people together and taught them what he knew from the Bible. When he had taught them all he knew, he sent a man across the island to look for missionaries, but none could be found. "Oh I think you, me lose, nobody come along you-me," he told his little group of followers. Then he thought a moment and added, "No matter white man no come and missionary no come. No matter, Jesus, He stop here!"

Even so, Samuel had kept his ears open for any news of missionaries. Finally the captain of a passing ship who was a Christian told him about the mission work at One Pusu. By now Samuel had seventy followers. He begged the captain to take him to Malaita on his return trip so that he could meet the missionaries and bring someone back to help teach his followers. The captain agreed, and Samuel finally made his way to One Pusu, where he begged for missionaries to be sent to his village. Soon afterward teachers and missionaries were dispatched to Samuel's village on the island of Guadalcanal.

When Florence heard about this she was amazed at the way a man with little learning could hold on to his faith without any encouragement or additional teaching. She promised herself that she would visit Samuel on her next visit to the Solomon Islands.

Chapter 15

Death and Hardship

It was not until July 1910 that Florence found the time to visit the Solomon Islands once again. During the time she had been in Australia, three people had been murdered at One Pusu, including a small boy, yet the work there was being enthusiastically carried on.

On this trip Florence sailed with her nephew Northcote on the *Evangel* around the island of Malaita. Their first port of call was Ai'Io, on the eastern side of the island, where they were to pick up Thomas Sandwich, one of three native teachers who were going to start an outpost on Rennell Island, one of the southern islands of the Solomon group. Florence was delighted to see Thomas again. He had been struggling at Ai'Io for four years, working hard among the natives there but with little to show for his efforts.

Nonetheless, when it was time for Thomas to board the *Evangel,* the people of Ai'Io surrounded him and wailed as he left. He promised to return to them if he could but explained that it was time for the Rennell Islanders to hear the gospel message as well.

Aboard the *Evangel,* Thomas joined the two other members of the pioneering team: Tommy Makira, a native of San Cristobal who loved to preach and who had accompanied Northcote on many voyages, and Andrew Kanairara, an intelligent student from One Pusu. Florence hoped that Andrew would pick up the Rennell Island language quickly and be able to help the other team members learn it.

The decks of the *Evangel* were stacked high with palm stems and timber to build a small house for the three men. The men knew they were welcome at Rennell Island, because Northcote had already made five trips there and the islanders had started asking him if someone would come and built a permanent outpost among them.

The *Evangel* headed southeast along the coast of Malaita in heavy seas. They sailed through the Maramasike Passage to the western side of the island and then set out for Marau Sound at the eastern end of Guadalcanal, where they sought shelter for several days, hoping that the strong winds would abate. Finally, on the morning of August 11, they decided to venture out into the open sea and make a run south for Rennell Island. The *Evangel* was met by mountainous waves, and after six hours of being battered by them, Northcote decided they should return to the shelter of the sound. As they turned, the winds became a howling gale and the boat was whipped from side to side in the waves. Heavy rainsqualls made it impossible to see land, and the last vestiges of daylight were quickly fading from the sky.

Florence prayed fervently that God would allow them to sight Marau Sound soon. Once night fell, it would be too dangerous to venture near the reef that surrounded the sound, and they would have to spend the night out on the treacherous ocean. Her prayers were answered when a break in a rainsquall allowed Northcote to find his bearings and maneuver the *Evangel* through the reef and into the shelter of the sound. That night and all the next day the wind howled, and huge waves crashed on the reef. But the following morning, conditions were a little better, and they decided to set out once again.

It was still a rough journey of twenty-eight hours, but as the sun rose on the second morning out from Marau Sound, they spotted the outline of Rennell Island on the horizon. As they got closer to the island, Florence noticed that there was no sign of habitation along the coast. Northcote explained that on his previous visits he had noticed this too. Everyone on the island seemed to live out of sight in the bush.

It was 5:30 in the afternoon before the *Evangel* sailed into a wide, sheltered bay on the south side of the island. Within minutes three canoes were launched from the shore, and strong arms were soon paddling them out to meet the boat. The first canoe to reach them contained Temoa, a teenage boy who had attended school at One Pusu. He was overjoyed to see the missionaries and invited everyone to come ashore immediately.

Florence was grateful for the opportunity to get off the boat and once again put her feet on dry land. She found Rennell Island one of the most beautiful spots she had seen in the Solomon Islands. The water was the clearest blue, and the beach consisted of fine, white sand that sloped up to a fringe of coconut palms. Florence took a deep breath and thanked God for getting them there safely.

Everyone Florence met seemed very friendly. Some of the children were scared at first, but curiosity about Florence's sun umbrella soon won them over. Before long they were racing up and down the beach using the umbrella like a sail.

Temoa had taught the natives they met some English words, which everyone was eager to try out on the missionaries.

Soon a man, whom Temoa said was the chief, came running down the beach. As he got closer, Florence noticed that he was covered in fine, blue tattoos and wore a bark cloth around his waist.

"Welcome," the chief panted when he reached them. "Kungava'im you welcome. Come see'im village."

Florence looked to Temoa questioningly.

"Good idea," Temoa said, approving the chief's suggestion.

"Housey no long way, come housey!" the chief insisted. Then he ran up the side of a steep cliff like a mountain goat. He stopped and laughed. "Missy, come housey come," he called to Florence.

Florence did not follow him straight up the side of the cliff. Instead she followed the track that wound its way up to where the chief was standing. By the time she reached him, she was out of breath. But the chief kept running on in front of her yelling, "Housey no long way."

Finally they reached a clearing, in the middle of which stood a structure with open sides and a single layer of leaves for a roof. Florence wondered what kind of protection the structure afforded when the monsoon rains whipped through, but she smiled at the chief. She walked around in the house but couldn't see a single possession in the place, not a cooking utensil nor a pot nor a stool. The only things the people appeared to own besides their bark clothes were tomahawk-like axes, which each man wore tied to a belt around his waist. Since there was nothing else to admire at the village, Florence headed back to the beach. The whole way back, the chief chatted to her in a mixture of pidgin English and the Rennell Island dialect. Florence could understand bits of what he said, and she understood when he told her how welcome the teachers would be on the island.

By the time the chief and Florence arrived back at the beach, the rest of the missionary group had unloaded the supplies from the *Evangel* and started clearing land for a small house.

Two days later the house was completed and the three native missionaries were ready to begin their new mission. As Florence said good-bye to them, she was sure that the next time she saw the three men they would have wonderful stories to tell. However, it was not to be.

Three days after the *Evangel* sailed away from Kungava and Rennell Island, the chief led a group of warriors who swept down on the new missionaries' house. They clubbed Thomas, Tommy, and Andrew to death and stole the supplies they had brought with them.

Florence did not hear of the killings for another two months, and when she did learn of them, she was devastated. Yet she clung to the hope that the three men had not died in vain. In a letter home, she wrote, "To human eyes this tragedy seems like defeat, while really it is a victory deferred. Some day the martyr's blood will reap a martyr's harvest."

The following year, in June 1911, another missionary was martyred. This time it was one of the European missionaries from Australia. Fred Daniels lived at Malu, but he traveled to the small village of Ailamalama on the eastern side of Malaita to help the local Christians there. Fred had been there for only four days when he was shot in the chest while singing the closing hymn at a church service. His murder, added to the three deaths on Rennell Island, rocked the mission, but no one was ready to retreat. In fact, Northcote went to New Zealand to recruit more workers. While he was there, he married Jessie Gibson and brought her back to join him on the *Evangel*.

Threats and rumors of violence followed on all of the islands of the Solomons, and Christians began to take refuge wherever they could. After seven local Christians were murdered in the tiny school at Cherith, the remaining students escaped to Nongosila, farther along the eastern coast of Malaita. When Florence heard of the incident she traveled to Nongosila to stay with the students and comfort them in their distress. A month later a missionary couple returning from furlough were able to take her place.

Relieved of her responsibilities at Nongosila, Florence returned to Australia to visit the new mission house located on Wynyard Street in Sydney. The place was just what the South Sea Evangelical Mission needed—a central location where goods could be ordered, correspondence sent out all over the world, and potential missionary candidates interviewed. The mission house was a joint venture with the China Inland Mission, and both mission groups shared the cost of running the place.

Florence was impressed with the workers who staffed the various mission stations throughout the Solomons and wrote several newsletters telling of the trials they were enduring in the islands.

In 1913 Florence once again returned to the Solomon islands and spent time at Baunani, eighteen miles northwest of One Pusu. A mission boarding school was now located there, and boys came from all over Malaita, the south coast of Guadalcanal, and San Cristobal to study there. One of the students in the school with whom Florence was particularly impressed was Andrew Ambuofa, Peter's nephew. He was a strong Christian and in line to lead his tribe.

Neither Florence nor anyone else was particularly alarmed when Andrew had a slight fever one Tuesday night. By the following morning, however, Andrew was dead. Everyone was stunned, and the other students from Malu insisted that his body should be taken back to their village to be buried.

Two men from Malu and six students offered to row a whaleboat carrying the coffin along the coast back to Andrew's home village. They set out at three o'clock that day. At eleven o'clock the following morning, three of the crew stumbled back into Baunani with a terrible tale to tell. A rip current had overturned the whaleboat, and since they were the only three who could swim, they headed for shore to get help. Meanwhile, the other five members of the crew clung to the upturned boat. Sharks circled the three as they struggled to get to shore, and crocodiles waited for them in the sand dunes. The three of them survived the ordeal and, as soon as they regained some strength, set out running for Baunani.

Another boat was immediately dispatched to search for the others, but no trace of them or the whaleboat could be found. This latest tragedy reminded everyone of just how much danger they all faced daily in the Solomon Islands.

Despite such setbacks, the work of the mission went on, and Florence continued to divide her time between the Solomon Islands and her support role in Australia.

In November 1913 Florence's youngest nephew, Norman, came to visit his brother Northcote in the Solomon Islands. Norman was a dentist and had a flourishing dental practice in Sydney, but when he saw the needs of the Solomon islanders, he decided to sell everything and join the South Sea Evangelical Mission. Florence was delighted to think that yet another member of her extended family was joining the mission.

In August 1914, just as World War I was erupting in Europe, Norman set out for the Solomon Islands. He went to serve at Baunani, where he relieved Clara Waterston, the missionary who had been serving there, so that she could return to Malu. Clara had been working with several Kanaka Christians to translate the Gospel of Mark into the Malu language. When Norman arrived, she was correcting the final proofs of the translation, of which the British and Foreign Bible Society had agreed to print one thousand copies. After she returned to Malu, Clara kept up her translation work, and soon Malu Christians had the entire New Testament in their language.

Just before Christmas 1914, Florence received word that her sister Emily had died. Although Emily's death was expected, as she had been ill with heart problems for many years, it was still a terrible blow to Florence to lose the sister who had been like a second mother to her. Florence could not help thinking back to the days when they sailed to England from New Zealand and Emily had to take charge of all the children when their mother became ill. What a wonderful job she had done, telling them stories and making up games for them to play. How long ago it all seemed now.

Florence and her two nephews and niece, Northcote, Norman, and Kathleen, who all served with the mission in the Solomon Islands, gathered to share their grief and mourn Emily's passing, They then pressed forward with the work of the mission, which they knew Emily would have wanted them to do.

Northcote had been telling Florence for some time now about the limitations of the *Evangel*, not that Florence really needed to be told. She knew that the vessel was too small to sail in rough weather and that Northcote and his crew could not reach the eastern coastlines of many of the islands during the monsoon season. Florence sent out a letter explaining the situation, and money for a new boat began to pour in.

With the money in hand, Florence returned to Australia to oversee the building of the new boat, which was to be a ketch-rigged yacht. The vessel would be seventy feet long and seventeen feet wide and would weigh thirty tons. The increased size and weight meant that it would have more deck space and two deck cabins.

While she was in Australia, Florence also oversaw the construction of a new mission house sixty-six miles outside of Sydney. The house was located in a quiet spot at Katoomba, in the Blue Mountains, and Florence knew it would be an ideal retreat for missionaries home on furlough. The bracing mountain air and majestic views would be a welcome change from the disease and stifling heat of the Solomon Islands.

As the year progressed, Florence was glad that both of these projects were under way. With World War I raging in Europe, building materials were in short supply and getting more expensive by the month, but Florence had been able to purchase enough materials in advance to ensure that both projects would be completed.

While World War I pushed up prices at home, it also stirred up more interest in missions. Soon Florence and her volunteer assistants found themselves mimeographing two thousand copies of Northcote's quarterly mission newsletter, which they addressed and stamped and mailed out all over the world.

Finally the new boat was completed. The *Evangel* was sold to an island trader, and the new boat commissioned. This vessel too was named the *Evangel*, and Florence and Northcote were pleased with her design and the way she handled in the water.

Another of Florence's nieces, Constance, also committed herself to work with the South Sea Evangelical Mission and went to serve at One Pusu.

Florence was delighted to learn that things were going well at One Pusu, where there was a constant need for new workers. By 1916, 130 students were enrolled in the eighteen-month-long teacher-training school located there. Despite the number of people wanting to become native teachers, the demand was still far greater than the number of teachers the school could train.

Many tribal leaders begged Northcote to send them workers. When they were sent to a place, these unpaid teachers led a simple life, starting tiny Christian schools and settlements and growing the food they needed to live on. Despite the hardships, time after time these teachers would return to the biannual meeting at One Pusu with stories to tell of how God had changed the hearts of the locals and how one by one the people were accepting the gospel. Florence was always excited by such news, though it meant that even more teachers would be needed. Another smaller teacher-training school was opened at Pau, in South Malaita, in 1917 to try to keep up with the demand for teachers.

At about the same time the new school was being opened, Grace Irwin, one of the older workers serving with the mission, died of blackwater fever. Northcote's wife, Jessie, also came down with the disease, but she did not die of it, though her recovery to full heath was very slow.

Regardless of the danger, more workers came from around the world to serve with the mission, some coming from as far away as Scotland.

Although she was now sixty years old, Florence continued to divide her time between administrative work in Australia and arduous trips to the Solomon Islands. By now she was ministering to the children and, in many cases, the grandchildren of the first Kanakas she had known at Fairymead.

Chapter 16

Her Real Legacy

When World War I ended in 1918, even more workers volunteered to join the South Sea Evangelical Mission. Among them was Florence's niece Constance, her brother Horace's daughter. At the same time, Florence's nephew Norman opened a new mission station at Star Harbor, on the extreme southeastern tip of San Cristobal. Meanwhile his two sisters, Joan, now also serving with the mission, and Constance, divided their time between teaching at One Pusu and visiting outlying areas on the *Evangel*.

Blackwater fever continued to threaten the health of the missionaries, and in 1921 Florence received the sad news that Northcote's wife, Jessie, had caught the disease again and died from it. After a brief trip back to New Zealand to visit his wife's family, Northcote returned to the Solomon Islands alone to carry on the work of the mission.

In September 1924 Florence was back in Katoomba when her brother Horace died. She wrote her thoughts about his death in a letter.

> Both he and my brother Ernest have been associated with the Queensland Kanaka and South Sea Evangelical Mission from the beginning at Fairymead in 1882. And through these forty-two years the work has had their sympathy and practical help and support. We will not see all of the results of his labors until we join him in heaven. God buries His workers, but carries on His work.

A month later Florence received another blow. This time it was her niece Constance, who had also contracted blackwater fever and died. She was buried at One Pusu. Florence read through some of Constance's old letters to her, and one in particular, written three years earlier from One Pusu, comforted her:

> This is a real battlefield, and I've got the soldier's love of battle very strong just now, and I couldn't leave my pals down here for a soft billet at home! They are so pitifully few already, and if I went home that would make one less to "carry on" the fight. And

that's why I have written so much home this time. I want you all at home to realize the *joy of conquest* as I feel it when I am sitting in school on Sunday morning and see the rows and rows of quiet earnest faces—brands plucked from the enemy's country and from his hand. It makes you realize, when you hear them singing and praying, etc., how infinitely worth while it is—even though it does cost, for some, fever, and even death. One thing that has been coming home to me lately is this, that you must be willing to die in this kind of rescue work. What does it matter if a few missionaries die in the attack? *You can't have real WAR without casualties*—if souls are really being rescued.

Florence comforted herself with the knowledge that Constance had died doing what she believed in.

At the time Florence was writing her autobiography and history of the mission. She had been asked to do so by a large English publisher, and she had already chosen the title, *Pearls from the Pacific.* She had been recalling so many positive experiences to include in the book as she looked back over the history of the mission, and these stories helped her through the bleak time of learning about Constance's death.

In November Florence wrote the last few paragraphs of the book. She ended with a summary of what the Queensland Kanaka Mission and the South

Sea Evangelical Mission had accomplished in the forty-two years since it had begun:

> Now there are 169 out stations. Meetings are held daily, generally both morning and evening. In some stations there is an additional day school for the children and on Sunday three or four meetings. All the Christians are expected to help, though there are usually one or two recognized leaders.
>
> God has given us exceeding joy in the ingathering and baptism of a great company of believers; 2,484 converts were baptized in Queensland and 3,716 in the Islands, making the total to November 1924 of 6,200 converts added to the visible church on earth.

It was an astonishing accomplishment for a shy girl who had started out teaching a few Kanaka men how to read at Fairymead, her brothers' sugarcane plantation in Bundaberg, Queensland. But Florence was not ready to rest on her accomplishments; there was still a lot of work to do. Regrettably, she was able to make only two more visits to the Solomon Islands. Her last trip was in 1926, when she was seventy years old. After this trip, Florence's body was too frail to take the pounding of the ocean voyage needed to get to the Solomons. But her heart always remained with the Solomon Islanders.

In her old age Florence settled into a small cottage at the back of the Deck family property in Killara, Sydney.

Although a new generation of missionaries had taken over the mission, Florence found great joy and satisfaction as she stayed as involved in mission affairs as she could. She loved to visit the mission house at Katoomba and attend the various meetings that missionaries home on furlough held in Sydney. As she entered her eighties, Florence still prayed daily for the South Sea Evangelical Mission and its workers, and she lived very modestly so that she could funnel as much money as she possibly could into the work.

On May 28, 1940, Florence Young died quietly at her home in Killara. She was eighty-three years old. Her funeral service was simple, just the way she would have wanted it, and she was buried at the nearby Gore Hill Cemetery.

In the months and years that followed, many missionaries traveling through Sydney visited her gravesite. But Florence would have told them that her real legacy could be found not in a cemetery but out in the remote and dangerous islands that made up the Solomon Islands, where the South Sea Evangelical Mission had by then recorded more than 7,900 conversions. Many of these later converts had never met Florence in person, but each of them knew her story well and owed her much. Florence Young had accomplished her mission.

Bibliography

Young, Florence S. H. *Pearls from the Pacific.* Marshall Brothers Ltd., 1925.

About the Authors

Janet and Geoff Benge are a husband and wife writing team with more than thirty years of writing experience. Janet is a former elementary school teacher. Geoff holds a degree in history. Originally from New Zealand, the Benges spent ten years serving with Youth With A Mission. They have two daughters, Laura and Shannon, and an adopted son, Lito. They make their home in the Orlando, Florida, area.

Also from Janet and Geoff Benge...
More adventure-filled biographies for ages 10 to 100!

Christian Heroes: Then and Now
Gladys Aylward: The Adventure of a Lifetime • 978-1-57658-019-6
Nate Saint: On a Wing and a Prayer • 978-1-57658-017-2
Hudson Taylor: Deep in the Heart of China • 978-1-57658-016-5
Amy Carmichael: Rescuer of Precious Gems • 978-1-57658-018-9
Eric Liddell: Something Greater Than Gold • 978-1-57658-137-7
Corrie ten Boom: Keeper of the Angels' Den • 978-1-57658-136-0
William Carey: Obliged to Go • 978-1-57658-147-6
George Müller: Guardian of Bristol's Orphans • 978-1-57658-145-2
Jim Elliot: One Great Purpose • 978-1-57658-146-9
Mary Slessor: Forward into Calabar • 978-1-57658-148-3
David Livingstone: Africa's Trailblazer • 978-1-57658-153-7
Betty Greene: Wings to Serve • 978-1-57658-152-0
Adoniram Judson: Bound for Burma • 978-1-57658-161-2
Cameron Townsend: Good News in Every Language • 978-1-57658-164-3
Jonathan Goforth: An Open Door in China • 978-1-57658-174-2
Lottie Moon: Giving Her All for China • 978-1-57658-188-9
John Williams: Messenger of Peace • 978-1-57658-256-5
William Booth: Soup, Soap, and Salvation • 978-1-57658-258-9
Rowland Bingham: Into Africa's Interior • 978-1-57658-282-4
Ida Scudder: Healing Bodies, Touching Hearts • 978-1-57658-285-5
Wilfred Grenfell: Fisher of Men • 978-1-57658-292-3
Lillian Trasher: The Greatest Wonder in Egypt • 978-1-57658-305-0
Loren Cunningham: Into All the World • 978-1-57658-199-5
Florence Young: Mission Accomplished • 978-1-57658-313-5
Sundar Singh: Footprints Over the Mountains • 978-1-57658-318-0
C.T. Studd: No Retreat • 978-1-57658-288-6
Rachel Saint: A Star in the Jungle • 978-1-57658-337-1
Brother Andrew: God's Secret Agent • 978-1-57658-355-5
Clarence Jones: Mr. Radio • 978-1-57658-343-2
Count Zinzendorf: Firstfruit • 978-1-57658-262-6
John Wesley: The World His Parish • 978-1-57658-382-1
C. S. Lewis: Master Storyteller • 978-1-57658-385-2
David Bussau: Facing the World Head-on • 978-1-57658-415-6
Jacob DeShazer: Forgive Your Enemies • 978-1-57658-475-0
Isobel Kuhn: On the Roof of the World • 978-1-57658-497-2
Elisabeth Elliot: Joyful Surrender • 978-1-57658-513-9
D. L. Moody: Bringing Souls to Christ • 978-1-57658-552-8
Paul Brand: Helping Hands • 978-1-57658-536-8
Dietrich Bonhoeffer: In the Midst of Wickedness • 978-1-57658-713-3
Francis Asbury: Circuit Rider • 978-1-57658-737-9

Samuel Zwemer: The Burden of Arabia • 978-1-57658-738-6
Klaus-Dieter John: Hope in the Land of the Incas • 978-1-57658-826-2
Mildred Cable: Through the Jade Gate • 978-1-57658-886-4
John Flynn: Into the Never Never • 978-1-57658-898-7
Richard Wurmbrand: Love Your Enemies • 978-1-57658-987-8
Charles Mulli: We Are Family • 978-1-57658-894-9
John Newton: Change of Heart • 978-1-57658-909-0
Helen Roseveare: Mama Luka • 978-1-57658-910-6
Norman Grubb: Mission Builder • 978-1-57658-915-1
Albert Schweitzer • 978-1-57658-961-8

Heroes of History

George Washington Carver: From Slave to Scientist • 978-1-883002-78-7
Abraham Lincoln: A New Birth of Freedom • 978-1-883002-79-4
Meriwether Lewis: Off the Edge of the Map • 978-1-883002-80-0
George Washington: True Patriot • 978-1-883002-81-7
William Penn: Liberty and Justice for All • 978-1-883002-82-4
Harriet Tubman: Freedombound • 978-1-883002-90-9
John Adams: Independence Forever • 978-1-883002-50-3
Clara Barton: Courage under Fire • 978-1-883002-51-0
Daniel Boone: Frontiersman • 978-1-932096-09-5
Theodore Roosevelt: An American Original • 978-1-932096-10-1
Douglas MacArthur: What Greater Honor • 978-1-932096-15-6
Benjamin Franklin: Live Wire • 978-1-932096-14-9
Christopher Columbus: Across the Ocean Sea • 978-1-932096-23-1
Laura Ingalls Wilder: A Storybook Life • 978-1-932096-32-3
Orville Wright: The Flyer • 978-1-932096-34-7
Captain John Smith: A Foothold in the New World • 978-1-932096-36-1
Thomas Edison: Inspiration and Hard Work • 978-1-932096-37-8
Alan Shepard: Higher and Faster • 978-1-932096-41-5
Ronald Reagan: Destiny at His Side • 978-1-932096-65-1
Davy Crockett: Ever Westward • 978-1-932096-67-5
Milton Hershey: More Than Chocolate • 978-1-932096-82-8
Billy Graham: America's Pastor • 978-1-62486-024-9
Ben Carson: A Chance at Life • 978-1-62486-034-8
Louis Zamperini: Redemption • 978-1-62486-049-2
Elizabeth Fry: Angel of Newgate • 978-1-62486-064-5
William Wilberforce: Take Up the Fight • 978-1-62486-057-7
William Bradford: Plymouth's Rock • 978-1-62486-092-8
Ernest Shackleton: Going South • 978-1-62486-093-5
Benjamin Rush: The Common Good • 978-1-62486-123-9
Dwight Eisenhower: Supreme Commander • 978-1-62486-142-0

Available in paperback, e-book, and audiobook formats.
Unit Study Curriculum Guides are available for many biographies.
www.YWAMpublishing.com

CHRISTIAN HEROES: THEN & NOW are available in paperback, e-book, and audiobook formats, with more coming soon!

www.HeroesThenAndNow.com